Farewell to Hype

The Emergence of Real Public Relations

Francis Xavier Carty

Able Press

To my students
and to
our many guest lecturers
from the public relations profession
who have been
my best teachers

Contents

Preface

STORYTELLERS and poets held an honoured place in ancient Ireland, passing on the traditions which now make up our cultural inheritance. Their gatherings were usually jolly affairs with plenty of drink and socialising, just like a modern press reception !

The first public relations people were also storytellers, passing on their organisations' traditions and ensuring a lively gathering with plenty of drink and socialising. But, those early days of press agentry, exaggeration, manipulation and puffery left their scars and, to many, hype, short for 'hyperbole', is still the trade mark of public relations, promising more than it can deliver and making exaggerated claims about organisations and their products.

Public relations is now of age and has to say farewell to hype; be aware of its position as a senior management function; say farewell to mere images and image-making and concentrate on the substance beyond the images.

Real public relations is far from the pestering of journalists with trivial and totally uninteresting stories. That is joke public relations, the public relations of yesterday.

Public relations, concerned with the effect of company behaviour upon reputation, is trying to move to a higher moral ground as guardian of the corporate conscience.

This is an ambitious, and, to some, a presumptuous claim for what ex-Fleet Street editor, Tom Baistow, has called "the fifth estate", and one can hear the sniggers of those like Malcolm Muggeridge who described public relations as "organised lying". But if public relations is to have a role in the business of the future, this must be it.

In Ireland there are growing numbers of students taking public relations courses and many organisations are becoming aware of public relations for the first time. To date, the textbooks have been British or American; so, here is the first from Ireland. There have been works on special topics such as media relations, by Terry Prone and Martin Tierney, and customer relations by Feargal Quinn, to mention a few, but none on public relations as such.

This book has expanded from eleven years of lectures to more than seven hundred students on the DIT Graduate Diploma in Public Relations at the College of Commerce, Rathmines and the Certificate of the Public Relations Institute of Ireland.

These are first words but definitely not last words. Many issues are merely raised, leaving deeper analysis to a later day.

In many instances, I have taken on board the views of my colleagues in the public relations profession, attributing them where appropriate. Apologies if I have got it wrong in any case, or left out somebody.

Finally a few points on style. I have preferred to spell out 'public relations' rather than use the abbreviation 'PR' which has acquired flippant, even derogatory, connotations, as well as being duplicated with proportional representation. In reference to the function within an organisation, I say that, for example, public relations does this, personnel does that, marketing does the other. This avoids tiresome repetition of clumsy compound adjectives, as in 'public relations department', 'public relations manager', 'public relations officer', 'public relations person', 'public relations function'. These fuller expressions are used only when necessary to avoid confusion.

Also, I have favoured feminine pronouns and adjectives when speaking in general, taking into account the reality that half of the human race and the majority of those entering public relations are now women.

Francis Xavier Carty
Sandymount
July 1992

<u>**Chapter One**</u>

What Public Relations really is: The Function

1. What is public relations ?

PUBLIC RELATIONS is just that, relations with the public, but in professional public relations the public is divided into many smaller publics or audiences. These include employees, the community, customers, consumers, suppliers, distributors, politicians, public servants, financial institutions, stockbrokers, shareholders, financial analysts, journalists and opinion leaders.

    Every organisation has audiences and therefore cannot avoid having public relations. The choice is whether or not to use it properly.

    The most commonly accepted definition of public relations is given by the Institute of Public Relations in the UK. It describes public relations practice as "the planned and sustained effort to establish and maintain goodwill and mutual understanding between an organisation and its publics".

    There are, however, many other definitions, from the obscure to the banal, even to the level that it is "whatever the individual practitioner thinks it is". Jon White, former director of the MBA course in public relations at Cranfield Institute of Management, London, has examined 473 attempted definitions, some trying to specify what public relations is, others describing aspects of professional practice.

Central to the best definitions are the ideas of relationships, communication and reputation, but none of the 473 published so far have embraced adequately the wider concept that has emerged with real public relations.

Public relations is the management of all relationships which are important to an organisation. Circumstances will determine which audiences, or sub-audiences, are most important and need priority attention at any time.

It is also the management of all communications within the organisation and between the organisation and its outside audiences. The purpose is to create better understanding of the organisation among its audiences.

Some people refer to these audiences as targets at which messages are directed. This can give the wrong impression of passive audiences waiting to be shot. Instead, they are expected to be responsive and to answer back.

Public relations is also the management of the organisation's reputation. It identifies the perceptions which are held of the organisation and works to inform all relevant audiences about organisation performance. It is concerned with developing a deserved reputation for an organisation, one which is based on performance. This reputation will not necessarily be favourable, but only as favourable as the organisation deserves.

Public relations nowadays has to be the conscience of the organisation, helping it always to act ethically and in the public interest and concerned with the effect of behaviour upon reputation. It is the eyes, mouth and ears of the organisation, seeing it as outsiders see it and providing information, seeking to increase awareness among important audiences.

Frank Jefkins holds that negative attitudes are the key issue and he sees the work of public relations as the gradual, not necessarily overnight, conversion of these negative attitudes to their positive counterparts - hostility to sympathy, prejudice to acceptance, apathy to interest and ignorance to knowledge.

The end result of managing an organisation's relationships, communication and reputation are that people's attitudes and behaviour towards it are influenced. The manager has to be a persuader - otherwise her communication is ineffective.

Public relations cannot fully achieve all of its objectives in the short term; building up and improving relationships, changing attitudes, means a continuous, sustained effort rather than a short, sharp campaign. It is not an ad hoc, firefighting activity but has to be planned in detail and carried out with precision.

The manager has a counselling as well as a technical role, advising the organisation on its public relations response to issues, anticipating and predicting what is ahead and ensuring that all audiences are taken into account. Too frequently, especially in a marketing-led organisation, the customer only is considered.

Public relations goes beyond the techniques of communications, not just carrying somebody else's message, but advising what it should be.

Public relations tries to balance an organisation's words and actions with its audiences' perceptions of it. Imbalance on the one side can mean insufficient recognition and an obstacle to achieving objectives; on the other side it can create expectations that are too high, resulting in disappointment with failure to deliver on the expectations. The profession has a bad reputation for hyping and promising too much and not being able to deliver.

The correct advice is always to tell the truth because lies are wrong and they damage the organisation. Also, they are usually found out and the liar is not trusted again. It is best to tell the truth, even when it is embarrassing. That does not mean, for instance, that the press reporter's questions have to be asked for her. The wise spokesperson will answer truthfully what is asked but not always volunteer what has not been asked.

The witness in court swears to tell the truth, the whole truth and nothing but the truth. Loyalty, confidentiality, and common sense dictate that public relations will not always tell the whole truth, but it must be sufficient truth for the message to be understood.

Organisations are like families and nobody expects members of a family to tell the whole world about every detail that happens in the home.

Public relations is strong, not weak. It does not give in to every pressure group. Nor does it always have to be nice to everybody. Every audience should be listened too but not always heeded.

Public relations is aware of the likely consequences of all decisions and actions, but does not have to advise the easy way out. Tough decisions may have to be taken and when flak flies it often has to be taken on the chin.

Public relations is tangible and real - relationships are real, communication is real and reputation is real. Difficulties under any of these headings mean real difficulties for the organisation, affecting performance and commercial success.

2.   Why public relations ?

PLANNED public relations makes all of an organisation's relationships work for it instead of leaving them to chance and being problems waiting to happen. These relationships exist whether or not attention is paid to them. Failure to communicate with staff, for instance, is an invitation to future trouble, as is failure to find out what customers want. It is less obvious, but equally important, that the other relationships should not be neglected either.

If relationships are not managed there is lack of direction and effort is wasted tackling the effects rather than the causes of problems. It is better to anticipate problems and, if they cannot be averted, to exploit them as opportunities.

Organisations need to communicate, but successful communication does not happen automatically. When there is a sender and a receiver, the message from one to the other does not travel automatically. The message has to be coded so that the receiver understands and responds and the most suitable medium has to be selected. That is where public relations is needed.

Important as public relations is in good times, it is even more needed in bad times. Prompt, accurate communication was not merely desirable, but vital for the Goodman group of companies when they collapsed in summer 1990, and for Irish Distillers when it was fighting off a hostile takeover bid in 1988, and for Perrier water when it was withdrawn due to benzene contamination. Failure by these companies to use professional public relations skills would have affected not just their profits but their continuing existence, their investors' savings and the jobs of their employees.

Staff communications are often the cinderella in public relations programmes, but failure to communicate can lead to inefficiency, reduced output, low morale, costly work disruptions, high staff turnover and other personnel problems affecting output, quality and public reputation.

The presence of competition also dictates that communication cannot be left to chance or dealt with in a haphazard fashion. The same receiver gets many messages and is confused. What makes one message stand out from the clutter so that it is received and acted upon ? How can it penetrate the mass of newspapers, magazines, radio, television, informal channels without professional presentation ? How can it be translated and tuned for each audience ?

Public relations is needed also because of the importance of reputation. People prefer to do business with an organisation which they understand and respect. They prefer one which is seen to be efficiently run, which treats its staff well, which cares for its customers, which looks after quality. There is increased public concern about corporate behaviour, whether it be in care of the environment, treatment of women, or response towards the Third World and this concern is affecting purchasing habits.

Public relations is an insurance policy as well as an incentive to act responsibly and responsively in the market place. Building up a good, deserved reputation is like money in the bank. One never know when it will be needed. Communication cannot just start when a crisis happens - good communication must already have been there over a long period. At times of crisis one counts one's friends, rather than looking for new ones.

The organisation which understands public relations and uses it properly will be more likely to do as it would be done by

B

because it knows its audiences and is sensitive to them.

One frequent reason given for not organising public relations, and for letting it take care of itself, is that it is too expensive. The price of the alternative is rarely considered. Can any good organisation afford not to have public relations ? It can be more cost-effective than other forms of communication because it is less wasteful; its message is framed to a specific audience. One page of advertising in the national newspapers on one day can cost more than 365 days of expert service from a consultancy. Also an experienced consultant can be added to a management team for less than it costs to employ a senior secretary plus overheads.

Public relations is often neglected because it is alleged not to have a bottom line value in the company accounts. Some performance can be measured exactly but it will never be possible to achieve a total measurement of such assets as goodwill and reputation. The reason why the customer passes one supermarket to deal with another which is seen to care and to have a human face does not appear in the books of either, but it is a reality. Can anyone, likewise, measure the exact impact which the management style of the chief executive and her team have on the bottom line ? Do the crime figures ever reflect offences which the Gardai prevented due to good community relations ?

All reasons for engaging in professional public relations fall apart if its objectives are not clearly spelt out and understood. Many organisations do not realise what public relations is. Their perceptions are wrong and they do not know what to expect. Every recommendation and activity must have a clear purpose related to overall organisation objectives. Otherwise, there will be misunderstanding. Lord Leverhulme said that half of the money spent on advertising was wasted but he did not know which half. All of the money spent on public relations can be wasted if there are not clear objectives.

Do organisations realise why they need public relations ? Do they take it seriously ? Not sufficiently, for in 1985 Wilton Research & Marketing conducted a survey for the Dublin consultancy, John McMahon & Partners. They covered the top financial institutions, state and semi-state bodies and the top 200 companies. 41 % had a formalised public relations plan, but the others had not. 56 % admitted that their activities were usually undertaken on an ad hoc basis, that is, in response to a particular occasion, problem or emergency. However, 48 % used a consultancy.

The January 1989 issue of the business magazine, *Aspect*, listed the top 1000 companies, plus leading financial institutions in Ireland. Each was asked to name its public relations consultancy or say whether the function was carried out in-house. 163 (16 %) named their consultancy and another 15 (1.4 %) said it was handled in-house. What about the other 82 %, even allowing for errors in the compilation ?

Public relations for public relations is needed if all people are to be convinced of its need. When one really understands it, one no longer questions its value. But, as with the preacher, missionary zeal is not enough to convince a sceptical audience.

Nor is it enough to say that public relations is a relatively new profession and will take time to be recognised. Other professions glory in their youthfulness and they are understood. Some years ago who would have heard about the new financial services, or information technology, or computer systems ?

There are professions which once had the recognition problem now experienced by public relations. As recently as the 1950s Peter Drucker was writing of companies who regarded management and organisation theory as luxuries they could not afford.

The gurus of marketing would seem to most people to have won their argument and made the customer centre of the corporate circle, but not necessarily so. Today, only one fifth of Irish companies have a formal marketing function.

Drucker also recalls that 400 years ago surgery was performed not by doctors but by barbers who, untaught and unlettered, applied whatever tortures they had picked up during their apprenticeship[1]. Doctors, observing a literal interpretation of their Hippocratic oath not to inflict bodily harm, were too ethical to cut and were not even supposed to watch. But the operation, if performed according to the rules, was presided over by a doctor who sat on a dais well above the struggle and read what the barber was supposed to be doing aloud in Latin. Needless to say it was always the barber's fault if the patient died and the doctor's achievement if she survived - shades of how public relations is regarded.

Public relations does not solve all of an organisation's problems. It is but one cog, and a very important cog, in the management machine. Nor, however, is it a mere placebo, administered as a cosmetic exercise. The role of public relations should not be exaggerated, nor should it be ignored.

3.   Public relations through the ages

PUBLIC RELATIONS may not be the oldest profession, but it is one of the oldest. Ever since people and communities have wanted to communicate they have used the skills of public relations, but it is only in recent times that these skills have been refined and integrated into a separate discipline.

Some techniques have been organised for longer than others - house journals for 150 years, government information services for 70 and documentary films for 50.

The Bible illustrates public relations in practice with the media of the day being tablets of stone and scrolls of papyrus. Moses, bringing the Ten Commandments down from God on the mountain is seen by some as the first public relations person. Others point to St. John the Baptist announcing Christ.

In Irish tradition the old storytellers (seanchaí) and the poets (filí) had a place in society similar to modern public relations. The medieval court jester was also a forerunner, able to tell the truth about the king and get away with it.

Famous campaigners won people to their ideas through convincing argument and suitable dramatisation and presentation, even when communication techniques were very primitive - the early Christians, Martin Luther and the campaign against indulgences, Daniel O'Connell and Catholic Emancipation, Wilberforce and the abolition of slavery.

The industrial revolution brought an expansion of industry

and commerce, especially in the UK and US. This created the need for manufacturers to communicate and make their products and services widely known.

Ivy Ledbetter Lee is usually credited as the pioneer of modern public relations. The son of a 19th century Georgia minister and a graduate of Princeton University, he started as a newspaper reporter. At that time organisations dealt with strikes and disasters on the basis that what they did was their own business and of no concern of the community. In 1906 he offered a specialist service to the coal industry which had had a series of damaging strikes. He said to the employers that he would improve their relations with each other and with the public and in particular with the press. But he insisted on dealing directly with top management and on being allowed to tell all of the facts if he thought it wise to do so. When, in the same year he helped the Pennsylvania Railroad Company after a serious accident, he broke all tradition by bringing the journalists to the scene in special transport.

Lee's approach worked. Media coverage, which had been hostile, soon became sympathetic and organisations realised that by being open they would be better understood. He told the newspapers that he was offering a service and if any of his material resembled advertising or propaganda they were to put it in the bin.

On the other hand, Lee was accused by some of manipulation and of identifying the public good with the good of big business against the interests of fair competitors. 'Poison Ivy' was one of his less complimentary nicknames.

The rise of Hollywood saw the coming of the press agent, a rather sleazy character, a propagandist who did no good for public relations. Films which featured these agents, often as caricatures, made the case worse.

The man who coined the term 'public relations', one of the giants in its early days was, and still is, Edward Bernays. Jewish, born in Vienna and nephew of Sigmund Freud, he was brought to the US as a one-year-old and is still alive and working a 12-hour day at the age of 100 ! His 350 clients have included four US Presidents, Calvin Coolidge, Woodrow Wilson, Herbert Hoover and Dwight Eisenhower, as well as the inventor Thomas Edison, the singer Caruso and the dancer Nijinsky. He refused his services to Franco and Hitler. In 1923, he wrote the first textbook for public relations, *Crystallizing Public Opinion*, followed by others including, in 1928, *Propaganda*. He quite happily linked public relations and the public good with manipulation, or engineering of public opinion, and with propaganda. Bernays started the world's first course in public relations, at New York University in 1923. His present consultancy rate is $1,000 dollars an hour.

In the UK, the Government was, by the 1920s, using public relations techniques to tell people about its health, pension and housing schemes. The marketing boards of the 1930s used public relations cleverly to place product publicity stories in the press, very much as recognised today.

When Ireland's new Electricity Supply Board (ESB) appointed Ned Lawler as its public relations officer in 1927 it was the first public utility organisation in Europe to have such a position. Lawler had been active in the War of Independence and was political correspondent for the *Irish Independent*.

The groundwork for a lot of modern practice in the UK was done in the war-time Ministry of Information. Many of these information officers formed consultancies when the war ended.   Postwar development of public relations was rapid. It became the concern of all - government departments, organisations involved in commerce, industry and the professions, businesses large and small, charitable organisations.

When the Institute of Public Relations (IPR) was formed in the UK in 1948 its first president was Sir Stephen Tallents, a pioneer of marketing board public relations from the 1930s. The Public Relations Society of America was formed in the same year.

The Public Relations Institute of Ireland (PRII) was formed in 1953 with Ned Lawler as president for the first four years. He was succeeded by Leslie Luke, public relations manager for Guinness.

Many consultancies were originally associated with advertising agencies, not a satisfactory arrangement because public relations was often offered as a free supplement to advertising and not seen as a function in its own right. The 1960s and 1970s saw a move away from this with more independent consultancies being formed.

Those still associated with advertising agencies tended to become separate companies within the group rather than public relations departments.

The emphasis has changed rapidly and will continue to change. The early history shows the dominance of media relations, reinforced by the large number of journalists who were recruited to the profession. Media relations will always be important, but only as one part of the service. Management skills are now required to a much greater extent.

New areas of specialisation have developed with the most lucrative in the past few years being financial, because of the growing number of public companies, and political, as the importance of getting through to the political and civil service decision-makers has been appreciated. The environment will be the big issue for the next decade and beyond.

So much has changed in the past twenty years, aided by new technology, that few would predict where the profession will be in another twenty years. It may be that the smaller companies, which cannot afford the major investments in technology, will be absorbed by the large ones. But, then it will always have to be a human service and it may once again be beautiful to be small.

4.   False ideas

PUBLIC RELATIONS has a bad name. Many people are confused about it, quite a few are hostile, and others are just cynical and derisory. The expressions "bending the truth so that people like you" and "organised lying" are used. The surprise is that the profession has been so unable to do a good job of public relations for itself.

People are confused about public relations. They don't know what it is and when pressed they see it as press relations, or as a form of advertising or marketing. Many young people wanting to enter the profession think it is all about talking to people and socialising. They think that they will be good at it because they "love meeting people".

When the French prostitutes had their classified advertisements banned from the back page of the *International Herald Tribune* they advertised themselves as specialists in public relations. Nobody protested. Did the French people care or was it all the same ?

Other people claim to know about public relations but are hostile to it. They see it as a somewhat dishonest activity and attribute every form of shoddy practice, con trick, whitewash and propaganda to 'PRs' or 'PR outfits'. They regard the public relations life as superficial, even parasitical, going from one dinner and reception to another, wining and dining journalists and floating on a cloud of stupid, hyped-up messages. Public relations has become unfortunately associated with hype and exaggeration. Journalists derogatorily refer to 'Hypeland', Wilson Hartnell managing director, Mary Finan being profiled in *The Sunday Tribune* as a 'Hype Priestess' (Happily, the article did not bear out the facile headline)[2] . If something fails or is seen to be a meaningless gimmick it is dismissed as "a PR exercise". If it succeeds and is praised there are few to hail the marvellous "PR exercise". Somebody else gets the credit. People who talk about "doing a PR job" usually mean covering up the facts, whitewashing the truth or fooling the general public.

Journalists are often cynical about public relations. Dubbed by Edmund Burke as the gentlemen of the fourth estate, they are conscious of their noble function to find out the truth and to report it as soon and as accurately as possible. But public relations is now the fifth estate because it can control most of the news and is often the only source for the journalist. This frustrates journalists and they don't always want to trust the source. They fear they are being manipulated and used; that there is a catch somewhere. They can be manipulated and they are frequently used because they have been made lazy by the amount of material which is fed to them. Michael Finlan of *The Irish Times* wrote about "the relentless and irresistible rise of PR", seeing the present scene as so different from when he started out. Then "attempts to suborn the press were somewhat lacking in delicate subtlety; they filled us with whiskey from a dirty glass and hoped we stayed conscious long enough to get the story into print....Now we almost have to call in the movers to get the cargo of handout junk back to the office".[3]

It is hard to blame some journalists for being cynical. Diary writers and social columnists get about a hundred invitations and other letters a day, mostly from public relations people and mostly worthless. Insult is then added to injury when a junior person from the company rings up not once but several times asking if they got the invitation and if they coming to the shindig. No is never taken as a final answer and the phone calls are always at the moment when the journalist is at her busiest.

Frank Jefkins has described the word 'image' is one of the curses of modern public relations.[4] Writings on the subject are flooded with it. We hear about 'projecting a favourable image', 'creating an image', 'image-makers', 'positioning an image', 'improving an image', 'handling an image'.

Image is a confusing concept. There are as many different images, or perceptions, of an organisation as there are people aware of it. Unless the organisation is practising mind control nobody can direct what image a person will form of it. If a person's image is a negative one, it means either that the substance is faulty or it has not been explained properly.

Image is also vague. When one speaks about image does one mean the true corporate personality, or the reputation, or merely a word-picture or a slogan ? To say that the British Conservative party is a caring party conveys a word-picture through a slogan, but it does not necessarily mean that there has been any substantial change in the party. The word-picture can change without any effect on the reality.

Image is only a reflection of reality and is superficial. Professional public relations looks not to the image but to the substance. It seeks to create a deserved reputation and to gain recognition for achievement. Honest public relations can only be concerned with a true image, a real mirror-image. But so often the idea of image is used to mean a false image, an attempt to confuse people, to pretend the reality is something other.

One understands what people mean when they refer to the image of an organisation. Advertising deals in very persuasive images and image-making but public relations goes deeper than the advertising image. It must communicate a more substantial message that can stand up to an informed response and hold itself in further discussion and debate.

A Chinese proverb says that you cannot carve rotten wood. So-called image-makers are often merely painting over the surface. What is beneath is rotten and it is soon seen to be rotten and public relations gets a bad name. While individual people might have faulty images because of incomplete knowledge, no amount of effort to 'change an image' will succeed unless the core of the house is put in order.

Public relations also gets a bad name because some people who work in it are untrained and unable to apply the most basic skills. Anybody can set up in business as a consultant, or be given a company job as manager, trained or untrained. Unlike other professions which have developed over the years such as nursing, medicine and law, public relations is not subject to public control. Licences are not required.

The PRII have laid down conditions for membership relating to training, experience and age but nobody is obliged to be a member and there is no ongoing examination of members to see do they really know what they are doing.

Public relations is different from advertising, which is the creation of the most powerful selling message at the most economical cost so as to reach the greatest possible number of customers or potential customers. Advertising is a vital selling tool and public relations can help it through creating an awareness which will make customers more receptive.

Public relations is not marketing, nor is it part of anybody's 'marketing mix'. Marketing too often sees public relations as promotions, or as publicity, influenced by the narrow vision of some authors anxious to 'guard their turf'.[5]

Marketing is the identification of customers and what they want and the supply of what they want at a profit. Public relations people are often involved in marketing, and have a major contribution to make, but their ambit is broader. It reaches also to the non-marketing audiences - employees, the community, politicians, shareholders, financial institutions.

Nearly everybody in business is now seen to be in marketing.

The customer has been crowned. And quite rightly so. The importance of marketing is so obvious that it is amazing that organisations for so long produced goods and services, just hoping for the best, but never knowing who their customers were nor what they wanted. Public relations, however, has its own objectives, which like the marketing objectives, contribute to the success of the organisation and neither should be in conflict. The psychological insights and communication skills of real public relations are vital in helping the marketing effort.

Public relations is not sales promotion. Advertising persuades the customer to buy the product but sales promotion brings her the final step. It is like bringing a horse to the water and then making it drink. Sales promotion adds value. It is an ancient practice, claiming its origins in the Garden of Eden when free knowledge came with every apple and Adam and Eve accepted the offer ! The package of cereal has an added value because there is a free competition on the back, the bottle of wine because a promotions person is offering free tastings.

Public relations is not a soft sell, 'below the line' activity. It is upfront and not below anybody's 'line' and it has to avoid being trapped in the language of marketing and sales. Public relations is about creating better understanding, seeking to change attitudes and behaviour, telling not selling. It can be argued, however, that while it is not about selling products it has something else to sell - an idea, an opinion, a change of attitude.

Public relations is not publicity, although it sometimes results in publicity. There is such a thing as bad publicity and some efforts are directed at minimising it or even towards keeping things quiet, avoiding publicity altogether.

Nor should it be propaganda, despite its early days, especially in the US. Basically, propaganda is the spreading of a system of belief or a set of values or opinions; it is a one-sided message, and not necessarily true, no matter how zealously believed by the propagator. Propagandists use the tools of public relations and they can be very good at it, but the function of public relations itself is to tell the truth objectively.

5.   Public relations as a management function

MANAGEMENT is the utilisation of people and other resources to achieve organisational goals. These are not exclusively economic goals, because management is needed also in non-profit and service organisations. The word management is also used to describe collectively the people who manage an organisation, as distinct from those who implement management policies and decisions.

Public relations is a management function because every organisation has to communicate and it is common sense that communications, internal and external, be as efficiently and as economically managed as any other function. The organisation that communicates inefficiently will not be understood by its audiences and will lose out both in its reputation and commercially.

The public relations professional is not only a technician, applying specialist skills and techniques, but also a manager, framing and influencing decisions which can affect all areas of organisation performance.

The importance of public relations as a separate management function is not always recognised. Look at a typical management structure, divided into finance, production, personnel, sales and marketing. Where is public relations ? - more often than not under the umbrella of marketing.

Public relations has a major relevance in the marketing function, but it cannot be confined there because communication, better understanding and reputation are also relevant to finance, production, personnel and sales. Public relations goes beyond the marketing department and the marketing audiences and, indeed, its advice may at times be different.

Napoleon said that every soldier carries a field-marshal's baton in his knapsack. In modern business, the marketing manager has a better than even chance of ending up as chief executive. But what about the public relations manager ? Is she seen as the perpetual court jester, a power behind the throne but never sitting on the throne herself ? And why ? Nowadays she is as skilled and as educated as any other manager. Do all public relations managers really believe in themselves as leaders or are they content to be faithful servants ?

Many organisation boards and chief executives see their public relations manager as the expert to help them with the press and get a bit of publicity for their products, but they would be as likely to consult her and listen to her before taking a serious decision as they would consult their barber before re-investing their pension fund[6]. The recognition of public relations in management is developing, but only slowly.

One reason for this lack of recognition is that it is difficult to put together a single set of skills and say that they are the package for public relations. People feel that they understand a training in accountancy, engineering, law or medicine, but they find public relations hard to define as a separate discipline because it is more correctly a group of disciplines. Also, the manager has often come from another media area, like journalism, and other managers find it hard to accept her as one of themselves. Training is still in its early days compared to other areas of management.

Every organisation decision has a public relations consequence. It is therefore sensible for the manager to be involved before decisions are taken and for her views to be considered along with all others. It is better to do this than merely expect her to pick up the pieces and engage in exercises of damage limitation after the event.

The ideal position for public relations in the management structure is beside the chief executive, with direct access, and not locked into another area with the inhibitions of having to deal through line management. The public relations role of the chief executive is most important and envelops the whole organisation and every function within it.

Keith MacMillan, professor of management studies at Henley College in the UK, sees public relations becoming increasingly a central management function which encompasses existing functions, such as marketing and personnel management, as well as the communications disciplines of traditional public relations, government relations and community relations.[7]

The communications function is often dispersed throughout an organisation. This does not need to change, but the role of public relations is to co-ordinate and ensure especially that everybody sings from the same hymn-sheet. Public relations does not have to be an empire within an organisation, but all doors should be open to it.

There often is a tension between public relations and marketing and advertising. It sees them as the ugly sisters with their big budgets and their often unconcealed contempt for cinderella. They have grown restless as cinderella has attempted to be taken seriously in her own right.

There should not be such a tension. The good organisation needs all of these functions and they need each other. There must be harmony or the organisation suffers and that is bad public relations. While they might come from different starting points and with different emphases in their communications approach, they end up in the same place, communicating messages to audiences.

Professional public relations has its own place and it does not need to be diffident or defensive. However, more than any other management function, it depends for its success on the calibre of the other management around it. If the organisation is badly managed, no amount of good public relations will remedy the situation. It is back to the Chinese proverb of not being able to carve rotten wood.

The public relations manager is the normal spokesperson for the organisation, especially with the media. But she is not the only one. Her role is to facilitate access to other management and to the chief executive, not to act as a shield behind which they can hide.

She must be the spokesperson for the whole organisation and not only one part of it. If she lets herself be used as a partisan in a dispute, representing only the management viewpoint, as against the trade unions, she becomes effectively a eunuch and loses credibility. This happens too often in present-day business.

The public relations manager has to have an independence that is not expected of other managers. While understanding and absorbing the culture of the organisation she must at the same time be able to stand outside it. She must be of the organisation and loyal to it but not an organisation creature. Her independence is vital to her professional respect.[8]

6.   Corporate Identity

THE CORPORATE IDENTITY of an organisation is the physical characteristics which distinguish it from other organisations. As with people, this identity is a reflection of personality. In an organisation, however, the corporate personality is different from the personalities of the many individuals who form it. People come and go but the corporate personality does not necessarily change.

As the personality changes, however, so does the identity to reflect the new reality. The Ford Motor Company and Guinness, for instance, are very different today both in personality and identity from when they were founded.

Corporate personality and identity can become identified with a strong individual who may be the chief executive. That can be good so long as she is there. But there will be confusion, at least initially, if she leaves or if she is disgraced.

The idea of consciously developing a corporate identity is not a new one. Kings of old had emblems on their shields and finally emblems became flags and soldiers wore uniforms. Priests and others developed distinct dress which marked them off from others. Napoleon, for one, was most conscious of the corporate identity of the armies which he led and of the symbolism attached to his deeds, as when he took the crown from the archbishop and crowned himself emperor.[8]

Corporate identity should be distinguished from corporate image. The identity is physical and it can be changed and controlled. It comes across the same to everybody. Image, on the other hand, is in the mind of the beholder and there can be as many images of the organisation as there are people aware of it and one cannot so easily change it.

Corporate identity can, however, affect the corporate images which individual people form. If the identity is confused, the image will most likely be confused. Some priests in recent years have moved away from clerical dress because it marked them off too much from the people to whom they ministered. It gave the impression that they were remote from the lives of ordinary people and their problems.

Corporate identity is more than appearances, it is a valuable resource which can be used for the commercial gain of the organisation. Correctly managed it can inspire loyalty, attract the best recruits, affect decisions, aid recognition and attract customers. The organisation that in all that it says and does presents a strong and confident identity has a headstart on its competitors. Coca-Cola has been shown in repeated surveys to be the most recognised brand in the world and its handscripted logo has been virtually unchanged since it was introduced in 1886. Some trade names impress so much that they become generic and are used unwittingly to describe the competitors, for example, hoover and xerox.

All organisations have an identity whether it is planned or not. The objective is to ensure that it is a true reflection of corporate personality and the nature of the business.

✕Establishing a new corporate identity and implementing all of its applications can be expensive. AIB paid an initial £1.5 million for the design and implementation of their new identity. They undertook it because the nature of their business had changed from traditionally narrow banking to more broad-ranging financial services and because they had expanded from an exclusively Irish base to become international. They launched it on 8 January 1990 and in subsequent press advertisements said: "As we start in the 1990s, we are signalling our readiness for the future and we're expressing this readiness with a new identity for the AIB Group".

These are the sort of reasons for which corporate identity is changed - new type of business, changes in structure and activity following a merger or a takeover, change of location. Also, it could be the sign of recovery after a crisis.

The change has to be total and it should not be piecemeal. It should take into account every manifestation of the organisation's identity - name, logo, company colours, letterheads and all other stationery, design of premises, labels, uniforms, advertisements, sales literature, newsletters, annual reports, corporate gifts and so on. Bigger and more well-known companies have to consider a greater number of details. In a group like Hilton Hotels there could be thousands of elements, down to every fitting in every corridor, to be considered. At its most basic corporate identity looks at every outward sign of the organisation.

A name can mean a lot with organisations as with individuals. Change of name can be very significant. Political leaders, film stars, writers and footballers have changed the names of their birth to suit better the job they were doing. But people are not fooled. British Nuclear Fuels changed the name of their Windscale power station in the face of mounting criticisms of it. It became Sellafield but most dismissed this as a "sellotape" job. Datsun motors changed their trading name to that of the parent company, Nissan and great expense was incurred to tell people about it.

People often identify the organisation by its logo, and this is one of the most vital elements in identity. It should be simple, distinctive and meaningful, but not be too complicated and it should in its abstract way say or imply qualities of the organisation. AIB's new four colour logo is distinctive but possibly too complicated. "Our new corporate symbol", they say, "is inspired by one of the earliest Celtic images of the Ark and the Dove. It is a symbol that reflects security, recognises our past whilst heralding a future where we serve different communities all over the world".

Bank of Ireland, for similar reasons, made a change. But unlike AIB they merely tidied up their 1971 logo, a change so slight that the ordinary public didn't notice it, whereas AIB made the launch of theirs into a big event which attracted media coverage and public comment.

Trade characters can be useful elements in identity, for example, Johnny Walker, the Bisto Kids, the Michelin Man, and Batchelor's Beany and Barney. And slogans can be distinctive. "Guinness is Good for You" is still familiar to people all over the world although it was dropped many years ago. Organisations run competitions for slogans because a good one can work wonders for corporate and brand recognition, giving a lead over competitors. The best slogans are simple, the sort that we think we could have thought up in our bath. They have a familiarity, a warmness, like "We compete - you win", for the new PMPA insurance company.

Another aspect of corporate identity is the mission statement, an American invention, which is catching on elsewhere. Generally it states "the way we do things" in a brief document which is often

c

publicly displayed and circulated to staff. Typically it describes the type of business, the services provided, the markets serviced. An abbreviated form can be the statement of core values which is more an expression of "what we believe in", the organisation's philosophy.

These statements can act as a beacon for the organisation, particularly when it is in a storm. They bring it back to basics - are the customers still number one, does management have an open policy towards staff, is quality always put before convenience ? They can provide guidance for the board of directors, the management and the people in an organisation and a vision and a direction with which people in the organisation can identify.

Among many other points, for instance, Bank of Ireland states that it is "to remain in the private sector" and "to maintain our independence". The international Dow chemical company says that its conduct "demonstrates a deep concern for ethics, citizenship, safety, health and the environment." Johnson Wax quote their founder who said "The goodwill of the people is the only enduring thing in any business. It is the sole substance...The rest is shadow".

If the organisation does not have a defined corporate personality, if it does not project a clear corporate identity, then the public relations manager must work on it. She is involved in corporate identity, not to design it, but to work with the designer and other professionals. One person, whether public relations, chief executive, personnel or any other manager, cannot decide alone what best portrays the organisation. It must be a consultative process. Otherwise the designer, who is not reared in the culture and traditions of the organisation, will fail to come up with the best identity.

All levels of staff should be involved and realise that they are involved. When First National Building Society changed their long-standing corporate identity, assistant general manager of marketing and development, Gerry Murphy said: "This is an evolution, not a revolution, the most important thing is that we bring the employees with us".[9]

There must be consistency, with the same message coming through every detail of the identity, consistency not just in design but in use. The new identity must be monitored and after a while adapted where necessary. It is good to have a handbook explaining the logo and other aspects of the identity and how they should be used in different circumstances.

A new corporate identity will not of itself stop a bad organisation being bad. In behaviour and performance it must live up to what it claims in its corporate identity and its mission statement. There should not be a gap between the organisation in its symbolic identity and its products and services. ✓

7.   Setting up the public relations function

IN SETTING UP the public relations function an organisation has several options. It can ignore it altogether; ask a staff member to look after it; recruit an experienced professional; engage a consultancy or combine the expertise of in-house and consultancy.

Ignoring it altogether is a prerogative of management. In the same way, other functions can be ignored like planning and budgeting, production control, personnel, marketing or getting oil for the central heating. As a consequence the business will not perform to its true potential.

The organisation which believes that it should appoint somebody but is not very convinced may select a problem member of staff because she is a good socialiser. They will expect her to be 'good' with the press, jolly and personable and able to shake them off an embarrassing story. That is not the way to do it; square pegs don't fit into round holes unless they are smaller than them - such a person will never be big enough for the job.

Selecting and training a staff member with good potential is another option. The end result may be good, but in the meantime, what will happen ? This person will be thrown in at the deep end and, lacking the support of professionals, may become disillusioned.

Some organisations use public relations as a path upwards for a promising manager. Regardless of specialist skills or knowledge of public relations she is believed able to do the job because she is a promising manager. This is like the conductor of an orchestra expecting a good violinist to play the trumpet at one concert and the harp at another - after all, you are a good musician and it is good practice for you !

Such a manager will lack professional confidence and probably remain ignorant because she is only a bird of passage. She may manage the department well because she is a good manager but she will be like a sailor moving deckchairs on the Titanic, unaware of what is going on below deck and out in the ocean. She will let public relations go by default unprepared to identify and exploit opportunities to communicate with audiences and strengthen corporate reputation.

Recruiting an experienced person should ensure the respect of other management because of proven track record. She will be active from day one and able to establish the department. She will be a good communicator, sensitive to reactions and attitudes, interested in management and business, efficient and well-organised, at ease with people, imaginative and enthusiastic.

If the organisation is small, the danger may be to seek a jack-of-all-trades and get somebody for public relations who is also expected to look after advertising, sales and marketing. Some stunt musicians can play several instruments at the one time through strapping them to different parts of the body. They are one-man orchestras - a novelty but not to be taken seriously.

If the organisation has insufficient activity to warrant a full-time manager of public relations it may be better to engage a consultancy. But the consultant must have direct access to the chief executive, because that is where public relations starts and finishes.

For many organisations the best arrangement is a consultant to complement the work of the in-house department, supplying the outside view and providing the specialist expertise which the in-house staff might lack.

The in-house manager is full-time and always available. She absorbs and understands the organisation's traditions and cultures, knows the internal communications lines and is trusted as "one of ourselves". On the other hand he may be too much of an insider and unable to apply the wider perspective. She may be locked into a structure of line management without proper access to the chief executive. She may become caught up in faction-feuding and promotion hassles.

The in-house manager must be allowed to get on with the job without too much interference or red tape. She must be informed and listened to before decisions are taken, for it is not enough to use her as an exorcist after the event. She can have problems with the chief executive's whims and temperament, but if she is to be effective she must be prepared to tell the emperor when he has no clothes. Public relations should be more than a set of ad hoc exercises in damage limitation.

The consultant brings expertise gained from handling similar work for other clients. She is not just an individual, she leads a team. Her office is usually convenient to print and broadcast media and to suppliers of specialist services. She knows these suppliers and can select the best for each job. She is paid for her time, usually at about £60 an hour. She cannot always be available instantly, but if she is well-organised somebody in her team will be on hand.

Irish consultancies are generally small and hard-working and have a reputation for good service. In the UK clients complain that they meet the front-line people when the contract is being pitched for but after that they are handled by a succession of junior people who move on rapidly and never really get to know the business.

Care should be taken with the choice of consultant because the relationship can break down, as in marriage, unless it is worked at. The reasons for breakdown are similar - finance, loss of interest, lack of attention, arrival of a more attractive partner[10].

The good consultant is accessible and available within reasonable limits. She is flexible and can develop a familiarity with the client's industry and way of doing business. She does not make empty promises but delivers punctually and efficiently on what is promised.

The good client listens to her consultant and keeps her in the picture. It is futile to withold information and then expect the consultant to handle an issue instantly as the media land on her doorstep. The motto on both sides should be "no surprises". The chief executive does not want to get first word of her organisation's problems on the morning news. Nor does the consultant want a call from the press asking for instant comment on a takeover bid when the client has not informed her.

The choice between in-house and consultancy is not one of which is better or cheaper. Circumstances have to be considered and they are not identical for any two organisations.

On average the spending on public relations is about 20 % of that spent on advertising, but the criterion should not be a percentage of such an unrelated budget. public relations should be costed separately, and priorities established to match short and long-term resources.

Consultants tend to have a higher profile because they have to make a profit and stay in business, but the number of people working in-house is greater. A 1985 survey found that 48 % of the top 200 Irish companies and state bodies used PR consultants.[11] This number had grown by 40 % over the previous five years and has continued to rise.

Consultants are frequently engaged through third-party recommendations rather than direct advertising. Sometimes an organisation asks a few consultants to present proposals, but there is now caution in responding to these approaches because some people fish for ideas and then use them without reference or remuneration to the consultant. When the consultant pitches nowadays it tends to be a presentation of credentials about her company and its executives, giving only an outline proposal following the initial brief.

When large consultancies pitch competitively for business, they are prepared to spend a lot of money on it because the rewards can be good. Hill & Knowlton's British head, David Wynne-Morgan, said in 1987 that 90 % of their business came through competitive pitches. On one occasion, for the Old Trafford Industrial Park, they spent £45,000 preparing their presentation, but it was worth £1.2 million in fees and they got it. They knew the risk was worth it once they had assured themselves that it was a genuine contest and that they were not going in just to be milked of ideas.[12]

Traditionally, consultants have not charged for preparation of proposals in cases where they did not win the contract. That is changing, however, and it is now normal practice in such countries as Germany and Switzerland, and spreading.

Whoever is asked to manage public relations must, however,

believe in the industry, the company and its products. It is silly to appoint an anti-smoker in a tobacco company, or a vegetarian in a meat factory. The analogy with the legal profession should not be brought too far; public relations must believe in the value of the case it is making and not just see it as a challenge to prove that black is really white.

8.   Planning public relations

PUBLIC RELATIONS is a planned, sustained management function, not a once-off or occasional exercise, nor a fire-fighting emergency tactic. It must be planned, costed and evaluated over an agreed period.

In professional public relations there should be no such thing as 'a PR exercise'; every activity should be directed to an audience to achieve an objective at the most economic cost.

Programmes are usually planned and costed on a year-to-year basis. They cover all anticipated activity but are flexible enough to allow for unforeseen events.

They may be prepared by in-house managers or outside consultants but, for convenience, we shall refer here to the experience of the consultant.

The first stage is to prepare a brief with the client, resulting from an initial letter or conversation in which priorities and current and anticipated issues are considered. For instance, the emphasis may be on adapting to sudden growth, restructuring after a takeover or merger, adapting to the new exposure as a public company, recovering from a crisis, expanding into new overseas markets. The consultant needs to know this background so that public relations planning may be consistent with overall planning.

The present position of the organisation must be analysed - previous public relations, its success or otherwise, attitudes held towards the organisation.

The consultant will undertake some private research to ensure that what the client tells her about the organisation is a true reflection of what its audiences experience. Journalists can be a good source for this information. Professional research into attitudes and perceptions is desirable before preparing proposals, but organisations are rarely willing to pay for it.

Objectives must be set out. They will vary from year to year, but should be as specific as possible. General aims should not be enough - they should as far as possible be translated into quantifiable objectives. For instance, the motorist driving out of Dublin may have the aim of driving to Cork and that might be sufficient if she is going away for a casual unplanned weekend. But if she is on a business trip she will be more specific. Her aim may be Cork, but she will have an objective there. It might be a cold call on a prospective customer in Patrick Street. Or she may be even more specific; an appointment with John Murphy at 11.30 to make a presentation to the board of the Murphy company.

Typical objectives in public relations relate to increasing awareness, creating better understanding, correcting negative attitudes, improving perceptions. They could be to help the company to recover its reputation after a disaster, make it better known following a takeover or introduction of new services, improve staff morale after a period of upheaval or poor industrial relations, put the company case to political decision-makers so as to influence legislation in a way favourable to it.

These objectives should not be absorbed into or confused with marketing objectives which might be to introduce a new product, sell into France, achieve 20 % growth in the home market, become the number one brand, find out how many customers prefer the twin-pack to the single-pack. Nor should objectives be confused with the means selected to achieve them. To publish a newsletter, for instance, is not an objective, but a means to communicate better with the people who will read it.

When the objectives are clear, it is easier to define the target audiences. These are typically employees, customers, the community, suppliers, distributors, the money market, financial institutions, politicians, other opinion leaders and numerous sub-divisions of each.

Priorities among audiences must be established. It could be employees at a time of company restructuring, customers when a new product is being introduced, the community when a new factory is being planned, the money market and financial institutions when a flotation is planned, or politicians when there is threat of potentially damaging legislation.

The next stage is how to communicate so as to match the audiences with the objectives. The consultant is like the doctor, using her knowledge of the medicines, in this case the communications techniques. She has a chemist shop full of techniques; her experience tells her which are most suitable in each instance. She will use a combination of them to prepare proposals, which are the heart of the programme.

It is important that she gets a feeling for the organisation, the environment in which it operates and what it has tried before. There may be good medicine, but too much of it might kill the patient; there may be medicine to which the patient is allergic.

An important strategy will often be use of the mass media, but selections have to be made - which media ? what mixture of national press, radio and television, or specialist trade press, or local media? Other media will usually be required - newsletters, brochures, conferences, meetings, special events, open days, sponsorships, exhibitions. In applying some of these strategies public relations will be working on its own; in others there will have to be close partnership with marketing, advertising and other specialist areas.

Public relations is a labour intensive activity and everything cannot be done at once. Unlike the strong, sharp advertising campaign, it is more gradual and sustained. The programme requires a timetable so that activities are stretched over the period rather than crowded into the first few weeks. Advertising can be in short bursts, public relations ideally goes on all of the time. The scheduled calendar of events means that maximum impact can be made with each, rather than suffocating the patient with everything at once. One does not throw in everything in the hope of achieving something. One very good proposal, adequately reaching the right audiences and achieving the proper objectives in a cost-efficient way, could suffice.

The programme has to be costed, the better the detail, the

better the value for money. The consultant charges at an hourly rate - which can be difficult to anticipate, but the exercise has to be done. The experienced consultant has a good sense of how much work each programme and each aspect of it might require. Further elements of cost, apart from the professional fees, are the materials used, and the outside costs such as hotels, travel, printing and hire of halls.

Finally, the programme should have some method of evaluation built into it. Nobody wants to spend money without knowing the return for it.

There are various models for the preparation of programmes. There is nothing sacrosanct about any one of them but the obvious questions should be answered, as summarised in the five Ws and H. What message is the programme trying to get across ? - consult the brief; why ? - the objectives; to whom ? - the audiences; where and how and when ? - detailed in the proposals and the budget.

The programme is presented to the client as a professional document, even if there is also a formal presentation. The reason is that it may have to be shown to other directors and managers before it receives final approval. It is therefore a selling document for the consultant.[13] It should be reasonably detailed, but not so much that the busy executive has not time to examine it. The tendency now is towards shorter documents with clear, concise information and recommendations. It should demonstrate that the consultant has understood the brief and is in tune with the mind of the company.

This detailed document is now rarely prepared until the consultant and the client have agreed in principle to work together and there has been a proper briefing, even a trial working period.

9.   Training

PUBLIC RELATIONS has been slow to develop the academic and intellectual base that other professions have built. Textbooks are often superficial and repetitive and fail to stretch the minds of students.

The practice of public relations is grounded in the findings and insights of management science, human behaviour, communication theory and so on. But it takes time, first to convince public relations people that there is such an underpinning and then to convince the business community and the general public. Public relations is, for many people, still a social, jolly sort of thing, wining and dining and persuading the press to publish a favourable news item or photograph.

Public relations is not so much a single discipline as a collection of disciplines, some theoretical, some practical. The good professional needs to acquire all of them and know how to mix them.

While practice alone makes perfect, training prepares for practice and ensures better quality performance, and sooner. Training separates those who are suitable from those who are merely enthusiastic.

The person who succeeds in public relations is, first of all, a good communicator, with both writing and speaking skills and able to use the new electronic media. She is a well-organised person, as public relations is so much about organising programmes and events and putting order into the approach of employers and clients. Also, she is reasonably outgoing but does not have to be excessively so. Ability to deal with people is important, but not the only thing. Too many come for course or job interviews with the idea that public relations is all about meeting people. They say that they 'love' meeting people and are good at 'one-to-one relationships' and are 'people' people. Further desired qualities are enthusiasm, a sense of humour, an ability to smile, resilience, imagination, initiative and loyalty. But loyalty, whether to one's own organisation or to one's clients, has to be tempered with reality. Truth cannot be compromised. The indefensible can never be defended.

Training in Ireland had a brief start at the College of Commerce, Rathmines in the 1950s and resumed on a permanent basis in 1978. The present one-year full-time graduate diploma in Public Relations admits 30 people each year, chosen from several hundred applicants. Graduates from the course have been employed by virtually every consultancy in Dublin and a number have gone on to set up their own consultancies and to take up senior positions in industry and the public service.

While Rathmines is the longest established course in Ireland and fully recognised by the Public Relations Institute of Ireland (PRII) as providing the educational qualification for full membership of the Institute, recognition has also been given to the BA degree in Communications at Dublin City University which includes a public relations option. Rathmines, in addition, is recognised by the Institute of Public Relations in the UK as an 'appropriate educational qualification' for membership.[14]

In 1986 the PRII started its own two-year certificate by night. Each year it offers approximately 120 places, from about 250 applicants. The course is directed mainly at people working in public relations or a related area. Many of these students are not expecting a full-time job in public relations, but are studying it because they and their employers realise its relevance to their existing work. Politicians, bankers, industrialists and civil servants have graduated from the course in addition to public relations executives and administrators, marketing, advertising and journalistic people.

The UK-based Communications Advertising and Marketing Foundation (CAM) has a certificate and a diploma programme. People prepare for its examinations either by private study, or correspondence or through one of more than twenty recognised colleges, including the University of Ulster.

University College, Galway, has a graduate diploma in Applied Communications, with options in journalism and public relations.

Occasional short courses, organised by the PRII and other organisations, deal with different aspects of public relations practice such as writing skills, TV and video, press relations, sponsorship and crisis management.

With the profession developing so rapidly, attention must be given to relevance in the preparation of syllabi and the design of courses, with constant revision to meet the changing realities.

The syllabi for the Rathmines diploma and for the PRII certificate are adapted from the Wheel of Education, a concept devised by Sam Black and first introduced by the International Public Relations Association in 1979 to show the best combination of skills and knowledge which need to be allied to the basic principles of theory and practice.

The Wheel of Education is arranged in three concentric circles. At the centre is the hard core of theory and practice, essentially what public relations is all about and how it happens. That explains the function and gives an understanding of the tools which it uses, the audiences whom it seeks to influence and the many contexts, or playing fields, within which it operates.

The middle circle identifies related skills which are needed in public relations. These include journalistic writing and editing, photography, television, radio and video production and printing.

The outer circle shows other helpful areas of knowledge - management, marketing, advertising, sales promotion, politics, law, finance, communication theory and social psychology.

These lists can be amended as the practice of public relations evolves but central to all syllabi is the communication function and the need to communicate to all of a company's audiences and create better understanding.

At present, the greatest need in practice is for writing skills. People in public relations spend more time writing than doing anything else and their skills must be as developed as those of the journalist. They also fulfil a key management function and must understand and be able to apply modern methods of management.

Teaching cannot automatically create a top professional; much still depends on personality and aptitude. But the right person, given the right training, can enter the business with a running start and be productive from day one.

The PRII has been progressive in recognising the need for training and giving its recognition to courses. It first laid down educational requirements for new entrants in 1984, several years before the IPR in the UK. The IPR had planned for entry requirements as far back as 1962 but hesitated, fearing it might not get any members !

There are now in Britain a number of degree courses in public relations. The University of Stirling, in Scotland, runs a full-time M.Sc degree which is also offered part-time by distance learning. The College of St. Mark and St. John in Plymouth has a master's in European Public Relations. CERP, the European Public Relations

Federation, is gathering information about courses and syllabi and preparing an approved list.

As public relations comes of age, its training also comes of age. It is part of the maturing process of any profession. Many Irish organisations still do not realise the importance of training for public relations and one still sees unqualified people appointed to important positions. When they fail, public relations itself is devalued in that organisation.

The alternative to training is the 'sitting-by-Nellie' approach, learning from the people beside whom one works. They may be excellent professionals but might not always have the time or the ability to teach properly. Also, one only learns what they know and one takes on board their bad qualities as well as their good ones.

In more relaxed and less cost-conscious times the sitting-by-nellie approach might have been effective but now everybody in the office has to be productive and Nellie no longer has the time. And also, one needs to be flexible and to know more than Nellie can pass on.

Training never ends. It is just the start of a lifelong process. It enables one to hit the deck running but to keep running one needs to keep an open mind and to continue learning. The real professional never ceases to be a student.

Thirty years ago few people would have attached much importance to financial public relations or to political lobbying and parliamentary public relations, or to environmental issues; few would have even guessed that desk top publishing would have the old professionals retraining in keyboard skills. Nobody knows with certainty what will happen over the next thirty years and what new flexibility and skills will be required.

It was estimated thirty years ago that the professional in an area like public relations had a half-life of twenty-five years. That is, if she knew to-day all that was needed to do her job properly, in another twenty-five years she would still know half of what was necessary and after another twenty-five years a quarter. Today the half-life is down to five years. Know all one needs to know today, but without further training one will in five years know only half of what is needed to do the job properly.

There has to be flexibility and realism in training. Structures have to allow the system to absorb a person from another profession who brings relevant skills and experience, but also to equip her with the skills which she lacks.

One future trend may be towards in-house training to complement the existing courses. The in-house training could be carried out by staff or by external personnel.

If companies only use qualified accountants, solicitors, architects, builders, doctors and other professionals, it is reasonable that they look to trained public relations executives, now that these are available in such large numbers. One doubts if any high-flying executive would board a plane knowing that the pilot was untrained, but with a bit of trial and error might muddle through.

10. Ethics

THE NEW emphasis on social responsibility is relevant to the public relations manager, because she is the conscience of the organisation. The good organisation no longer just makes money but behaves responsibly towards its staff and the environment and always acts in the public interest. The public relations manager must at all times be prompting it to do this.

A new study[15] highlights growing consumer pressure for corporate accountability. It gives instances of 'ethical purchase behaviour' and how consumer boycotts can bring a major corporation to its knees. The organisation that does not behave itself is now losing out in the marketplace.

While the public relations manager is in some ways like a lawyer who makes a case for her client, the analogy cannot go the whole way. The lawyer can defend an obvious murderer and try to get her off, but public relations has to be on the side of the public.

Veteran consultant, Alan Campbell-Johnson says: "The ultimate responsibility of public relations is to the public interest, on the basis that the public interest must be in your client's interest - irrespective of short-term factors. If you don't advise a client firm where it is going astray you are failing in your responsibility"[16].

One should refuse to work for an unethical client so long as the unethical behaviour persists. As a public face for that organisation public relations is obliged to be familiar with all aspects of its behaviour and it is not good enough to plead ignorance of the ugly side. As a major source of an organisation's information to the mass media and to other audiences, she must be uncorrupted and seen to be so. She cannot allow herself to be a shield for a corrupt management, nor be a spokeswoman who bends the truth, or tells lies.

Journalists will forgive incompetence, indeed in their cynical way some of them expect that, but they will never forgive lies. The liar will be blacklisted. They might not tell her, just freeze her out and ignore her. She will wonder why she does not get coverage any more.

It is better to say nothing than to tell lies. At the end of the day lies will be found out, so that it is not only ethical to tell the truth but also common sense and commercial sense.

Public relations is frequently accused of news management and manipulation, even corruption of the media. Organisations may be selective in what they say, they may tend to highlight the favourable news, but like a family, they will not necessarily tell the whole truth about what goes on behind closed doors. It can be unwise, but not necessarily unethical, to be economical with the truth, but in public relations the trust of the media is at stake and once lost it is rarely regained.

"The first casualty when war comes in truth", to quote US Senator Hiram Johnson in 1917, but perhaps the first casualty is really public relations. Much is made of inaccurate coverage and media bias in time of war but it is often the public relations people who, at the behest of the generals, strangle the media and use them as a propaganda arm.

Despite instant, nonstop television coverage, access to the truth has not been improved for the war correspondent since the tame journalists of World War 1, selected by their governments, reported the Battle of the Somme from a distant hill as a great victory with few losses.

Public trust is vital for public relations. British consultant, Tim Traverse-Healy describes it as "the cornerstone of our existence

- and its success. The outside world is prepared to grant us this success, but we will be judged on our professional standards of behaviour and practice"[17].

International codes of ethics warn public relations against corrupting the media of communication. What happens in war, frequently in off-the-record, non-attributable briefings, can easily become corruption worse than the wining and dining of journalists to plant a favourable story with them. But journalists, and their editors, are now questioning whether this hospitality is ethical. Surely the news should stand up on its own without a dinner to go with it, or a trip to the West Indies ? When one is bought a dinner, can one really remain unbought oneself ? Is it correct that an airline should offer a journalist a ticket, with the cost to be reimbursed when he returns and mentions that airline in her story ?

The reaction against 'freebies' is leading to new codes of ethics in newspaper offices. More journalists are now refusing free travel and hotels, preferring to go on press trips only if their papers pay for it themselves.

The Public Relations Institute of Ireland, along with other European associations, requires its members to abide by The Code of Athens and The Code of Lisbon.

Athens, from 1965, sets out basic principles which nobody could dispute. Lisbon, from 1978, amended in 1989, goes into more detail and relates more to daily experience.

Lisbon looks at professional standards and qualifications and emphasises honesty, intellectual integrity and loyalty. It then considers professional obligations and the importance of being open and honest. For instance, all clients should be represented publicly and competing clients should not be taken on without the consent of both parties.

All activities should be open and identifiable. One should declare on whose behalf one is acting. In the past there have been British MPs who were in the pay of foreign governments as lobbyists but did not inform Parliament and then spoke, say, on a motion proposing sanctions against that country.

Lisbon endorses the practice that one is paid for time and materials, and not on commission. There is debate at present on this

D

point. It is not demanded in the US where firms often advertise that they handle media relations on a results-only basis.

The implications in payment on the basis of achieved media coverage are obvious. One cannot guarantee media coverage, for in any reputable publication that is the prerogative of the editor. The practice implies the danger of dishonest deals with journalists.

Lisbon bars consultants from engaging in unfair competition with one another. They may advertise their services but not 'poach' clients. All direct approaches to competitors' clients are forbidden. Some see this as too gentlemanly and they want it removed. Poaching happens, but it is usually discreet and through third parties, rather than blatantly knocking on doors.

The difficulty with codes of ethics is that they bind only the members of the governing bodies and are rarely enforceable by law. An unlicensed profession like public relations cannot be policed so long as practitioners remain unregistered. Current concern, especially in the UK, centres on the growth areas of political lobbying and financial public relations. Many in these fields are not members of the national professional bodies and there is some concern that their methods might be harming the public interest.

Insider dealing in the Stock Exchange and the relative ease with which it can happen, has caused concern about public relations and other advisers to public companies. In 1986, Anthony Franco, president of the Public Relations Society of America, was forced to resign when accused of insider dealing.

Public relations people are often defensive because of accusations, especially by journalists, that they are dishonest and have a somewhat shady pedigree, immortalised in many Hollywood movies by the sleazy press agent. It is encouraging that a US survey[18], undertaken by the Pinnacle Group, Inc., an international organisation of independent public relations firms, asked 795 business people to rank 16 professions on the basis of their ethical behaviour. Public relations came a respectable fifth, behind accountants, dentists, doctors and officers of large corporations. But they were ahead of advertising practitioners (eighth), newspaper reporters (eleventh) and politicians (fourteenth). The politicians were ahead only of TV evangelists and used-car salesmen.

11.   Public relations in a crisis

A MAJOR crisis with loss of life, disruption to work, damage to reputation and prolonged legal tangles can happen to any organisation at any time.

It will always be unexpected, usually sudden and at an inconvenient time. The Townsend Thoresen ferry, *Herald of Free Enterprise*, sailing from Zeebrugge across the calm waters of the English Channel, sunk with several hundred casualties outside the harbour. It was a Friday evening when staff at head office had gone away for the weekend leaving only two people in their press office. The Raglan House gas explosion in Dublin killed two people and damaged an apartment block. It was at 9.30 am on the morning of New Year's Day. An oil tanker, *The Betelgeuse*, exploded at the Whiddy Island terminal in Bantry Bay with 50 deaths. It was after midnight on a Sunday in January.

A survey of chief executives in the US, conducted in 1985 by Stephen B.Fink, president of Lexicon Communications, found that 89 % believed 'a crisis in business as inevitable as death and taxes'. Only 50 % admitted they had a plan for managing one.[19] When ITN News asked Townsend Thoresen what their procedure was for an emergency such as the sinking of a ferry, they replied: "This sort of thing never happens".

It is essential to communicate properly in such a crisis so that the minimum of pain, discomfort and concern will be caused to people and the minimum of damage inflicted upon the organisation and its products and services.

The notoriety and damage caused by crises often remains long after they happen. Places like Chernobyl, Lockerbie and Bhopal pass into popular currency and are forever identified with the crisis which made them famous.

The first move in crisis public relations is to anticipate by drawing up a list of all possible crises and planning how to respond. Crises include air crashes, explosions, fires, product fault, product contamination, terrorist attacks, kidnaps and financial scandals. A crisis can happen to even the best organisation because it is not necessarily something within one's control.

Public relations should be closely involved at all stages in anticipating, preparing for and handling a crisis because a crisis essentially involves relationships with important audiences, communication and the reputation of the organisation and its products.

Have a written crisis plan which can be implemented immediately and instinctively so that all communications will be co-ordinated and effective. It is an extension of the idea of fire drill with which people in all offices and public buildings are familiar. Make sure that everybody involved knows their role in the crisis plan and in particular have a crisis team whose responsibility will be to trigger it off. This team is on 24-hour 365-day shift.

In larger organisations it will be necessary to rehearse this plan with all playing their roles and journalists, relatives, police, fire brigade, etc being played by actors. No amount of planning can be guaranteed to prevent every crisis but one result of proper groundwork can be to avert some crises which might result from faulty practices and procedures. Henry Kissinger has said that an issue ignored is a crisis ensured.

What should be done when the crisis happens ? The plan immediately comes into operation and a cascade system of phone calls brings all the pieces onto the chess board.

Assuming that it is a major crisis with loss of life, like an air crash or an oil-rig explosion, there will be an operations room where all information will be centralised and charted. Linked to this will be the press room, staffed by public relations with immediate access to all other senior management.

The organisation must be seen at once to be acting confidently and to be in charge. It is important that there be one credible spokesperson and that all public statements be channeled through her. She could be the public relations manager, but the ideal is the chairman or the chief executive.

The first 72 hours after the crisis breaks are the most crucial. That is when credibility is made or destroyed. The media are there with space waiting to be filled. People want to know what has happened. If the organisation does not speak confidently, other sources will fill the gap and instead of fact there will be rumour, possibly inaccurate and certainly damaging. Instant "experts" appear as soon as a crisis occurs and their comments, usually disparaging, and often ill-informed, can dominate the media.

Exxon behaved appallingly and then communicated even worse in the Valdez oil spillage in Alaska. Chairman Lawrence Rawl delayed one week in acknowledging the spill and lost media control. He refused even to visit the site for a fortnight. The commercial result was an immeasurable loss in sales with many customers exercising "ethical purchasing behaviour" and transferring their business.

Crisis-planning exercises are more than cosmetic; there are vital human issues at stake. If life has been lost, relatives need information, consolation and reassurance. They need to know they are dealing with a human organisation which cares and will look after them. It is important that the spokesperson expresses genuine regret and sympathy over what has happened, even if she cannot yet supply all of the facts. She must be seen to care and that is where Michael Bishop, chairman of British Midland Airways, won praise for his statements at the plane crash near Castledonington which killed 44 people.

It is also important that the public be reassured. When a gas explosion in 1987 damaged a block of flats at Raglan House in Dublin and killed two people, there was widespread panic because Dublin Gas did not know what was happening and did not give any impression of caring. There was not any spokesperson available and it took nearly 12 hours for the company to issue a statement, which it later had to retract. There was confusion - unforgivable in a body providing a public, and potentially dangerous service.

Dublin Gas, in financial difficulty, had closed down its public relations department some months previously, because management regarded public relations as a luxury. In panic they then hired a consultancy, but that was after the explosion when their reputation was irretrievably in tatters and the whole of the city was in panic over the safety of the very old gas network into which new natural gas had been piped. The consultants, Wilson Hartnell, did an excellent job in damage limitation and press comments sought by the Public Relations Institute of Ireland confirmed this[20]. Some confidence was restored in the company, but public fear was not allayed and the sales of gas suffered greatly. The property market reflected it in the drop in prices for gas-fired apartments. The only refuge for Dublin Gas was the final restructuring which saw its takeover by the state body Bord Gais Eireann shortly afterwards.

At time of crisis the media need information. They need facts. The organisation which is prepared has up-to-date information kits for immediate release - details about the airport, the plane, the training of crew etc.

At times of crisis the spokespeople must confine themselves to facts, as many as they can possibly give. Avoid speculation - leave that to the media. The question of liability for damage can be tricky. There will usually be a clash between the legal and public relations people, the one insisting that nothing be said for fear of prejudicing later enquiries and court cases, the other insisting on as full a disclosure of the facts as is possible, also in the interest of protecting the organisation and the public[21]. British Rail, after 30 people died in a crash at Clapham near London, immediately admitted responsibility and made initial payments of compensation. This was important because the families of the dead and injured were worried about hospital and doctors' bills and loss of earnings. The company realised at once that it was responsible because of a signalling fault and saw no reason to pretend otherwise.

It is impossible to give too much information at time of crisis - the newspaper space and radio and television time waiting to be filled can be immense. Also, it is better to get all of the bad news out at once, rather than let it trickle out over days or even weeks. It is also better that the organisation tell its own bad news than that rumour be allowed to take over.

The spokespeople should be available to the media at all times during a crisis, even if there are no new facts. Have definite times for briefings, even if there is no new progress but just to show that there is nothing to hide. The spokespeople must have sufficient authority and not have to refer questions of fact back to a superior.

Part of the expertise is timing. Know when to wind down the operation. It could be as long as three months, but don't prolong it unnecessarily. Judge when media interest has subsided.

The international media are only interested in high-profile

crises for a day or two before moving to another trouble spot, but the national media remain longer and the local media until absolutely nothing more is happening.

The same principles apply to product faults and contamination as to violent and sudden accidents. In 1982, Johnson & Johnson had to withdraw worldwide stocks of their Extra-Strength Tylenol analgesic capsules when vandals tampered with the packs, injected cyanide and killed seven people in the Chicago area. It cost the company $100 million but when the product returned in triple-sealed, tamper-resistant packaging, there was renewed confidence and the brand recovered 80 % of its market share within a year of the tragedy. The culprits were never caught.

The principle in withdrawing stock is that it must return improved in such a way that the problem cannot recur. It is useless taking the product off the shelves and returning it unchanged a few days later. Total recall is not always the solution.

Another form of crisis is financial. The most high-profiled in recent years has been Guinness after the Distillers takeover and the jailing of chief executive Ernest Saunders with others. Guinness Ireland minimised spin-off by distancing itself from the embarrassment of the parent company and stressing its independence and separate management.

Crises mean round-the-clock activity and the disruption of all normal work and life. Everybody is involved. There is no rest for days and even weeks. The mechanics can be mind-boggling. That is where the consultancy can be of further help. When benzene traces were found in Perrier water, their UK consultants, Infoplan, handled the recall of 40 million bottles and the enormous recycling problem and relaunch. Daphne Barrett, chairman and chief executive, Infoplan, said that 5,000 calls from the media were logged by her company, 7,000 from the trade, 15,000 from consumers and more than 100 from scientists, engineers, chemists and universities. All of this was over a six-week period. Within six months of relaunch, the product had recovered 75 % of its UK sales.[22]

Some organisations resist the cost of planning for a crisis. Like Townsend Thoresen, they insist it can never happen to them. Michael Regester has suggested that the cost should be taken from the marketing budget.[23] It is small compared to the cost of launching and maintaining a brand, but overnight the total marketing budget can be wasted if a crisis occurs and is not properly handled.

12. Evaluation

PUBLIC RELATIONS can be expensive, with consultancy rates at around £60 an hour and senior in-house managers earning salaries in excess of £30,000 a year. It is reasonable that those who spend the money should look for evidence that it has not been wasted. Lord Leverhulme said that 50 % of the money spent on advertising is wasted, but that nobody knows which half. How much money spent on public relations is wasted ?

Advertising awoke earlier than public relations to the importance of research on which it could base advice and judge performance. It would be hard nowadays to accuse advertising of wantonly wasting that other 50 % of its budget. However, the increased spending on areas like direct marketing and sales promotion as well as public relations, instead of advertising, may be an indication that Leverhulme's other 50 % has been identified.

Public relations cannot continue to argue vaguely that it deals with intangibles like goodwill and reputation and that these can never be measured. That is not good enough for budget-conscious organisations. It does not convince them when they see public relations as the first luxury to be axed.

It is true that goodwill and reputation cannot always be properly measured and they are the concern of public relations, but for too long this was an easy way out. It must be demonstrated to management and to clients that proper research into awareness, attitudes and all of the other public relations issues are necessary as a foundation for proper advice and action.

Why should management expect to get its advice off the top of the consultant's head on the vague understanding that she has done all of this before, when they seek reports, statistics, feasibility studies and so on before they enter a new market, build a new factory, buy a new computer?

One measurement which plagues public relations is the amount of media coverage obtained. Since many managers use public relations primarily to get media coverage they see this as a measure and comparisons are made with the advertising cost of getting the same quantity of space or air-time.

Media coverage, but never volume alone, can be a measure of some public relations activity, especially in the area of marketing support. Extensive coverage on an inside page of an obscure publication which does not reach the target audience may be less effective than a smaller amount on page one of the publication which every one of that audience reads and respects. This confusion can be heightened in organisations where press clippings are photocopied, pasted on to separate pages and sent around to senior managers.

The comparison with advertising space is naive. Advertising space has its price, but editorial space, in a respectable publication, is priceless and it should not be possible to buy it. Readership surveys show that editorial coverage has three times as much credibility as advertising.

If the concern is with awareness and attitudes, the tone of media coverage will be more important than the amount. So, when assessing media coverage or trying to judge public relations by it, look first at what one is trying to achieve through public relations and then see not just the quantity, but the location and the tone of the coverage. Over and above this, and more difficult to find out, did the correct message reach its intended audience and were attitudes and behaviour influenced ?

Some organisations are at times concerned to keep their names out of the media. Is their public relations then wasted if there is not any coverage of their personalities and their activities ?

One reason for difficulty in measuring the contribution from public relations is that it is mixed so often with contributions from other functions. If a new product is a success it cannot just be the result of good public relations; other management functions have played their part - production, marketing, sales and so on. It is easy, however, for public relations to be the scapegoat for failure. And it is the fault of public relations that so often it is unable to defend itself.

Public relations often fails to be measured properly because objectives have not been properly thought out or have not been specific. If ones does not know what one wants to achieve, how can one know when it has been achieved ?

What is the price on ideas and advice ? What is the price on a successful exercise in crisis management, or on its failure ? What is the price on a political lobby which averts or changes legislation which would have been damaging or restrictive to the organisation's activities ? What is the price on a good internal communications system?

Paul Winner argues[24] that performance in public relations will be difficult to measure so long as public relations remains confused about what it should be doing. "More than any other aspect of management, public relations defies attempts to derive a below-the-line figure for any given activity", he writes. "While the basic philosophy and rationale behind public relations are still so shrouded in confusion and ambiguity, attempts to define or measure its contribution are doomed. Is it the purpose of PR to create a situation where economic performance of the organisation is likely to be enhanced ? Or is PR concerned with non-economic indicators: attitudes, perceptions, beliefs, motivations, habits, expectations ? Is any concern with the latter seen merely as a strategic route to achieving the former, or are these things valued for themselves ?"

The International Association of Business Communicators (IABC), at their annual conference in London in 1987, debated a motion that "it is possible to specifically measure the value of public relations communication programmes against a company's bottom line". The motion was narrowly lost, but there was some discouraging talk by delegates which pushed public relations back into its dark ages of vagueness and waffle. Some argued that it was not possible to measure effectiveness in this way, others that it was not necessary and one even claimed that public relations had more to do with world peace and goodwill between men than it did with business, profit and loss.

In the frequent absence of resources to conduct proper research on programmes before and after, the rules of thumb are a mixture of experience, observation and informal testing. What changes have affected the situation which was assessed before the programme was drawn up ? Some of these may be quite visible, others may only be discovered through desk research or talking to samples of target audiences.

Many admit that when a programme or an event has been completed, there is rarely time to sit back and think because something else is now happening and both client and consultant are preoccupied with it. Often the project is considered satisfactory if it has been completed on time and within budget and if generally the client feels happy about it and believes that her objectives were achieved.

Organisations and individuals often take action because something is wrong and there is unrest; the fire brigade is only called out when there is a fire. Political lobbyist Myles Tierney claims that all government action in a democracy is directed towards maintaining public repose.[25] The evidence of repose restored is indication that the action has been successful. For instance if the electorate are clamouring for a change in the law and it is seen to be a good measure, the Government acts. Repose is restored. Likewise a public relations programme can sometimes be assessed off the cuff, through the restoration of repose, but this cannot continue to be good enough if public relations is to be respected as a management function.

The dilemma about evaluation will remain with practitioners often asked to justify expenditure for results which will not be measurable against this year's trading performance. Jim Pritchitt, an Australian consultant, and 1992 president of the International Public Relations Association, has argued that "the most important measurement standard of all, and the one that the profession has to come to grips with, is satisfying the expectations it creates. Too often managers are allowed to have, or are given, unrealistic expectations by public relations practitioners, which simply are not satisfied by the activities then developed. That gap, between expectation and performance, is one which practitioners must close to gain better acceptance as a management tool. That is the real measurement of success in management - fulfilled promise, and satisfaction that what is being done is worthwhile for the organisation"[26].

Notes

1   Peter F. Drucker; *The Practice of Management*; Pan Books edition, London 1968, p. 233.

2   Lorna Donlon; *Hype Priestess*, The Sunday Tribune, 5 April 1987.

3   Michael Finlan; *The Relentless and Irresistible rise of PR*, The Irish Times, 4 October 1985.

4   Frank Jefkins, Public Relations Techniques, Heinemann, London, 1988, p. 64.

5   Philip Kotler and Gary Armstrong; *Principles of Marketing*, 5th edition, Prentice Hall International edition, Englewood Cliffs, New Jersey, 1991. Kotler has misled a whole generation of marketing people with his inaccurate perception of public relations and this latest edition is still misleading but there are signs in the overall treatment that he has matured somewhat. However, he still sums up public relations as "gaining favourable publicity and creating a favourable company image", p. 469.

6.   Niall O'Flynn, MPRII; *Managing the In-House PR Department*, Lecture to students of the Public Relations Institute of Ireland, April 1991.

7   Keith MacMillan; Lecture to eighth annual conference on Corporate Affairs and Advertising, London, 1987 (Reported in *PR Week*, 5-11 March 1987).

8   Wally Olins; *Corporate Identity*, Thames & Hudson, London, 1989, Ch. 1.

9   Interview,*Sunday Business Post*, 22 April 1990.

10   Tim Halford; *Commitment and time to prosper*, PR Week, 2-8 July 1987.

11   Already referred to on p. 6. Survey commissioned from Wilton Research & Marketing by John McMahon & Partners.

12   David Wynne-Morgan; Lecture to annual conference of International Association of Business Communicators, London, July 1987.

13   Jim Walsh; Lecture to Diploma students in Public Relations, DIT College of Commerce, Rathmines, November 1991.

14   From 1 January 1992, the seven appropriate educational qualifications for full membership of the IPR are: CAM Diploma in Public Relations; BA Hons in Public Relations, Bournemouth Polytechnic; Diploma in Public Relations, College of Commerce, Rathmines, Dublin; BA in Communication, Napier Polytechnic, Edinburgh; BA Hons in Public Relations, Business School, Leeds Polytechnic; BA Hons in Public Relations, College of St. Mark & St. John, Plymouth; MSc in Public Relations, School of Management, Stirling University.

15   N.Craig Smith, *Morality and the Market,*, Routledge, London, 1990.

16   Alan Campbell-Johnson interviewed by Robin Cobb, *PR Week*, 29 March 1990.

17   Tim Traverse-Healy, in debate, *PR or Propaganda - the Dilemma*, at Eleventh International Public Relations Association Congress, Melbourne, May 1988.

18   Report in *Communication World*, San Francisco, USA, October 1989.

19   Michael Regester; *Crisis Management*, in Pat Bowman (ed), *Handbook of Financial Public Relations,*, Heinemann, London, 1989, p. 99.

20   *Dealing with the Media in a Crisis - A Study of the New Dublin Gas Approach*, prepared by the National Council of the Public Relations Institute of Ireland for circulation to its members, 1987.

21   John McMahon, Lecture to Diploma students in Public Relations, DIT College of Commerce, 1991. Several insights in this section emerged from this and other lectures given by John McMahon.

22   Daphne Barrett, chairman and chief executive, Infoplan International, in lecture to conference, *Managing in a Crisis*, organised by Walsh Public Relations Ltd and The Sunday Business Post, Dublin 1990.

23   In discussion at above conference, *Managing in a Crisis..*

24   Paul Winner, *Effective PR Management*, Kogan Page, London, 1987, p. 71.

25   Myles Tierney, *The Parish Pump*, Able Press, Dublin, 1982, p. 74.

26   Jim Pritchitt, *Communication World*, IABC, May 1988.

Chapter Two

How Public Relations really performs: The Tools

13. Ideas

THE TOOLS, or techniques, of public relations are well-known. On display they can be compared to a plumber's bag or, more grandiosely, to a pharmacist's shop window. There lie all of the means required to do the job.

The difference lies in the ability of one person to apply the remedies properly, where another would flounder. The person with training, experience and skill knows which tools to use and in what measure and at what time.

In theory, anybody can cure a person coming into a pharmacist's shop with a pain in the head. Just apply every medicine in the shop until the headache is cured. But by then the patient will be dead. The professional knows at once which of the many cures will work quickly and efficiently.

Every manager is aware of the tools used by public relations and some think they can apply them themselves. But, as business life does not allow for long trial and error, it is better to get the professional who knows at once what to do.

Added to training, experience and skill the public relations professional needs another quality to put her ahead of the field - imagination. She must be an ideas person, as well as an expert on the nuts and bolts. She must have an extra instinct which enables her to look at an issue and come up with a new solution.

Ideas without purpose are merely gimmicks and public relations is rightly criticised for such gimmicks. However, there is no reason why business should not be fun, and it is quite in order for public relations to involve a bit of eye-catching novelty, so long as everybody knows the target and it is achieved.

Publicity is not an end in itself, but a means to achieve another end. Some ventures attract publicity and comment because of their novelty and human interest but it is very hard to relate them to the organisation responsible for them and to see how they contribute to any of that organisation's objectives.

The proof of a good idea is that everybody imitates it. There are only a small number of techniques and as soon as somebody applies one of them in a new way, the rest of the herd follow. Public relations is as derivative as any other business.

When a sponsor had the idea of presenting a big cheque to charity, literally as a big cheque, everybody cheered. The photographers had a new angle and the media responded by publishing photos of the large cardboard cheques bigger than the smiling participants. Everybody got in on the act and had to try to be bigger. When the Chrysler Corporation in the US was paying back to the Federal Government the largest-ever loan ahead of time, its charismatic boss Lee Iacocca arranged for the cheque to be the biggest of all time, constrained only by the difficulty of fitting it into the hotel elevator.

Somebody else had the idea of an annual flower day for charity, say to buy a daffodil for a pound and aid cancer research. An excellent idea and well deserving of support, an idea which caught the public imagination. But when there are days for every flower in the botanical gardens and for every fruit in the forest the idea runs flat. The first there, quite deservedly, retains its position of eminence but the others experience diminishing returns.

Engaging the world's top musicians to record a song together at Christmas to aid famine relief in Ethiopia was also splendid and succeeded. But, if it were happening every week, or even every Christmas, for every deserving cause, there would be less response.

Extending the Christmas record idea to a simultaneous world-wide concert was logical, but quite correctly, Bob Geldof and his colleagues knew it would only work once. The excellence of an idea does not mean that it can be repeated indefinitely. That excellence often lies in its novelty, the shock impact it can make on its target audience.

During the Dublin Millennium celebrations in 1988, a theatre group from Galway, called Macnas, got publicity well above their merits, through building a giant Gulliver. What more natural and more camera-grabbing than a giant Gulliver shipwrecked and washed ashore on popular Dollymount Strand in Dublin and being looked at by the little people of Lilliput. Every newspaper covered the event, it was a news item in its own right on television. It provided a day out for the family as children climbed up the giant arms and legs. Then Gulliver, or his replicas, had a few more days out - used in Dublin parades and then converted into a raft which sailed down the River Liffey. It was also appropriate because Jonathan Swift, author of *Gulliver's Travels*, was a Dubliner and spent most of his life in the city.

Centenaries can be pegs for civic celebrations. Dublin's 1000 (nobody was sure what it was meant to commemorate, except that 988 was the first time that taxes were levied on the already well-established Viking city), followed Galway's 500 and Cork's 800 and preceded Dundalk's 1200 and Limerick and Athlone's 300.

If these celebrations succeeded in focussing civic pride and led to improvements in the cities, encouraged business investment and brought more tourists, then they had a value and were a suitable public relations tool, but the impact is greatest for the person who gets the idea first. The year 2000 will create an orgy of celebrations and will be the peg for thousands of ideas. One won't have to be a christian to join in the celebrations.

When Pepsi-Cola launched their product in Ireland 40 years ago they flew a streamer from a low-flying small plane. It probably had not happened in Ireland before. We all looked up. We all tried the product. To-day, nobody pays any attention. No football match is complete without a plane with a streamer advertising something or other.

In 1989 the independent radio stations came on air. Century, which had a national franchise, went for some gimmicks to publicise its launch. Realising that many listen to the radio only in their cars, they had cabaret dancers on platforms at busy road junctions. It was a dangerous gimmick because it could distract drivers, especially males.

The motor industry realised long ago that it needed something more than a car to attract male buyers at exhibitions. So they draped smiling women across the bonnets. Every manufacturer and distributor soon did it. People came at first to see the smiling model, but afterwards attention was only caught in proportion to the amount of clothing she removed.

Imagination can gain attention for an event which would otherwise be quite ordinary. Each evening in Dublin there are numerous events, openings, launches, meetings scrambling for the attention of the newspaper columnists. Jury's Hotel in Dublin, top of the market, expensive and associated both with serious business and international cabaret acts, put televisions into the men's toilets, to follow their established practice of pinning newspaper pages above the urinals. The extra novelty was that their public relations consultant, Mary Crotty, held the press reception in the toilets. A good gimmick, it got plenty of coverage and photographs and people were talking about Jury's for some time afterwards. And, of course, they had to come and see the new televisions with the up-to-the-second market prices and details of movements in the money markets.

Ideas are not only the concern of public relations and marketing, they are part and parcel of the whole communications mix. The National Safety Council has one stunning advertisement which shows more than four hundred dead bodies with blankets over them on a country road. "They thought they were going home, they weren't".

Indeed, the creative people in advertising agencies must be among the most valuable people in business. What they can make out of an ordinary product, such as an anonymous bag of washing

E

powder and how they can dramatise it and convert it to the appropriate media; how they know when to annoy us so much but keep our attention so that the name sticks somewhere in our minds. Over the years one is tempted to be cynical and say that as television has tried to please the masses the programmes have become more banal and dull and the advertisements are all that are now worth watching.

Ideas can be generated by people sitting in their baths, or waiting in the traffic, but they can be prompted by brainstorm sessions, a regular practice in public relations offices. Put all of the staff in a room together. Let their ideas flow and assign somebody to record them without inhibition or prejudice. The client might never know some of the outlandish thoughts that emerged but somewhere in the mix she could be the winner.

The tools are limited but there is no limit to the imagination with which they can be applied.

14. Writing skills

WRITING, the basic tool of public relations, is essential in the application of the other tools. More time is given to writing than to anything else.

Writing skills need to be stressed even more in public relations than in journalism because public relations has to be more versatile. A newspaper columnist or a high court reporter may settle into a groove and only have to produce one form of writing for the rest of her life, but in public relations one has to be able to move at ease through numerous styles of writing, even in the space of one afternoon.

Here are 32 forms of public relations writing: news stories, news releases, captions, headlines, announcements, minutes of meetings, reports and proposals, feature articles, newsletters, invitation cards, press advisory notes, letters, advertisements, brochures, interview notes, radio texts, video scripts, video synopses, points for speakers, speeches, summaries of specialist documents, notes for exhibition catalogues, text for display material at exhibitions, posters and wall charts, educational leaflets and folders, instruction leaflets, instruction manuals, calendars, pocket and desk diaries, company histories, induction material, questionnaires.

Writers do not have to be born that way, they can be made. Writing is a skill which can be learnt. There have been raw recruits barely able to write their names. They will never win the Booker Prize for literature, but by diligent observation and practice they have acquired basic writing skills. Ironically, many people in public relations are bad writers.

One learns to write by writing. Even the most experienced author can suffer blockage before the blank page in her typewriter, or more commonly nowadays, before her blank computer screen.

To start, one should get moving and avoid being too obsessed with rules. Start filling the page. When finished, go back and improve, chipping here and there, like a sculptor, until one is satisfied.

The greatest writers revise their work. Writing can always be improved, but the realities of daily deadlines mean that it can only be as good as the time available allows it to be. Some of Cardinal Newman's original manuscripts show words crossed out five times, often ending with the original word restored. The true artist is never satisfied; perfection is the ideal, but only the fool ever believes herself to have achieved it.

Many journalists write best in their early years when they take more pride in their work and are still in awe of the printed page with mass circulation. As time goes on they become so practiced that they can nearly write in their sleep and some of them do. Their reputation and their grasp of subjects increases but the care with which they sculpt their finished canvas is reduced.

Apart from learning to write by writing it is important to know what you want to say. The 19th century British writer, Matthew Arnold wrote: "Have something to say, and say it as clearly as you can. That is the only secret of style". It is better to err by being too simple than by going over the heads of your readers. It is not insulting to them to write as if they are twelve-year-olds.

There is a lot of bad writing, particularly by people in specialist fields. And that is not surprising. Doctors may be good doctors but when they write down the results of their latest research that does not ensure that they know how to write. One often feels inadequate at being unable to understand a piece of writing; don't despair, it does not mean automatically that one is stupid, it is more likely that the author cannot write.

People who teach writing are often themselves poor writers. Do all teachers of English write well ? Who wins the essay prizes ? Is it the pupil with perfect grammar, writing about obscure oriental topics and using big words. People wonder if a degree in English literature is the best preparation for public relations; it proves one can read, but not necessarily write. Training in literature and criticism often ruins the ability to write clearly.

There can be guidelines for good writing, but it is a mistake to become imprisoned by too many rules. Studying grammar may not necessarily be the best way to improve writing. How will one ever conquer the tyranny of the empty page if one sees it first as a minefield of rules and regulations ?

Great writers are masters of grammar and not its slaves. They know when to break the rules and they appreciate daily usage. Purists have always lamented the demise of the English language through ungrammatical usage but still it survives, although some-what different from the English of Chaucer.

For instance, one is told not to begin a sentence with "and" or "but", nor to end with a preposition, nor to split an infinitive. And that is something which I would not want to always put up with !

Here is a simple ABC of good writing; A for accuracy, B for brevity and C for clarity and cohesion.

Journalists should be surprised at bad writing from public relations people but they will forgive it. However, they should not forgive inaccuracy, despite the low standards which some of their own have reached. The public relations person is the source of information and her accuracy must be unquestionable. Don't leave anything to chance. Check, check and recheck. Facts must be true, names and places must be spelt correctly.

Some years ago the editor of the *Irish Independent* suspended one of his sub-editors for an inaccuracy. The poor man, on being told that Fr. Patrick Smith was dead, consulted the Catholic Directory and wrote a brief obituary note. Sadly, he had killed the wrong Fr.

Smith.

Such high standards no longer apply and if journalists were suspended for such breaches nowadays papers would never be published at all.

The *Irish Independent* on 30 March 1991 carried an Easter message from Bishop Donal Murray, displayed strongly on its main feature page with his photograph. Unhappily, they announced him as Bishop Donal Kelly in 24 point type. Underneath, they had a poem written by Professor Brendan Kennelly of TCD. He was by-lined as Brendan Kenneally from UCD.

B is for brevity. Short words, short sentences, short paragraphs might be tiresome in a novel where the pace has to be varied but in normal public relations they should be the norm. Writers can learn from papers like the *Daily Mirror*, where some of the best journalistic writing has appeared.

Never use five words when one would suffice, e.g. write "now" instead of "at this moment in time". Make every word work and avoid, in particular, adjectives which are empty of meaning, e.g. past memories, true facts, absolute perfection, future plans, personal beliefs. Avoid adjectives like "unique" and "revolutionary" and be careful with "new", because they have lost their impact. What is unique any more in a revolutionary world jaded with new gimmicks? Prefer the simpler word, e.g. end, not terminate; begin, not commence; find out, not ascertain. When finished a piece of writing, read and re-read, trim and trim again.

C is for clarity. Bad writing comes across to the reader as turgid and awkward. She does not immediately know why, but she instinctively pushes on and does not make a further attempt to understand. Grammar may be devalued but there is merit in a sentence which contains a subject, verb and object, a sentence which moves from the known to the unknown, a sentence which prefers the active to the passive voice. Exceptions will be made for reasons of emphasis, but they should be exceptions.

Public relations writing should not be like a detective story; one should not have to wait until the last line for the answers. Business readers are not prepared to wait, they want to know at once what is being said. Therefore, say it without frills. If the company has lost £10 million and is making 500 people redundant that must be said straight off and without hesitation or ambiguity.

Clarity suffers when verbs are used as nouns and are qualified with empty adjectives, or when nouns are used as adjectives. For instance, which of these two is more clear: "There has been an affirmative decision for programme termination" or "They have decided to end the programme" ?

Cohesion applies to the way in which sentences and paragraphs are strung together. There must be a logical flow. The reader cannot take jumps in thought back and fro across the page. There must be a clear point, even if it is not always in the first paragraph. Somewhere in the page of say, a set of proposals to the managing director, there must be a sentence which could be taken out and used as a telegraph to define exactly what the writer is trying to say. And that point must lead to another point.

The public relations writer has to be flexible, moving in a single day from the punchy, no-nonsense approach of the press release, to the more discursive development of a set of business proposals and back to the crisp invitation card asking the Taoiseach to attend an exhibition of paintings.

15.   Media relations

"ASK NOT what your country can do for you, ask what you can do for your country", said John F. Kennedy. One might likewise describe the role of the press officer: "Ask not what the media can do for you, ask what you can do for the media".

Good public relations means being active towards the media, coming forward with information that is interesting and relevant. It means being honest at all times with journalists, not spoofing, not over-promising and not lying.

Truth is the basis of good public relations and of good journalism and it would seem that the two professions should work well together. But it is not always so. Tensions can arise when journalists feel that public relations is polishing the information or blocking them from the interesting angle. Public relations must not be seen as a buffer.

There was a romantic notion that journalists explored virgin territory digging for nuggets of gold. They called them news stories and faithfully brought them back to their readers.

Not so any more. When they reach their buried treasure nowadays more often than not they meet the smiling public relations person already there with the nuggets cleaned and parcelled in attractive presskits. They are assured that there is no further gold, but still they want to look for it. Sometimes they find clay and like to think it is gold.

Journalism is good for democracy; indeed journalists are the only real opposition to many governments. Edmund Burke, speaking in the British House of Commons in the 18th century, observed three estates in parliament, the lords spiritual, the lords temporal and the commons. But, pointing to the newspaper reporters' gallery, he proclaimed: "Yonder sits the fourth estate, more important than them all".

To-day, as veteran British editor Tom Baistow, has observed, there is a fifth estate, the public relations profession. Is it now more important than them all ?[1].

Tension between public relations and the media is healthy. It keeps both parties on their toes - the disingenuous manager who is determined to hide information or give disinformation and the lazy journalist who too easily takes everything she is given.

Some journalists do not like to acknowledge the help they receive from public relations. One resents Christmas cards which "thank him for his help" during the year. He insists that it is not his job to help public relations but to serve his readers and to ensure that they get the truth, whereas public relations tries to keep the real truth from him.

Pierre Salinger, White House press secretary during the Kennedy presidency, gives five principles for good media relations: facilitate access, facilitate coverage, establish credibility, make personal contact, maintain personal contact[2].

The first two points recall Ivy Ledbetter Lee. Make it easier for the media to cover the story, even if it is bad news. Bring them to the scene of the rail crash, fly them on the presidential plane for a foreign visit. Then facilitate them in every possible way and help them to get their stories back in time. At a major event, that can mean providing offices, refreshments, telecommunications links and anything else that is needed.

Public relations facilitates the journalist but its exclusive access to and control of news can very easily turn it into a manipulator, only releasing what it pleases and how and when it suits the organisation. The organisation's timing is not always the journalist's timing. The journalist might want the information now, the organisation might want to hold for a few days until more pieces fit together to create a balanced story.

If the story gets out sooner than the organisation might have wished, the best advice is to co-operate with the enquiring journalist. She is probably going to use it anyhow, so it is best to get one's view in straight away.

Credibility can take a long time to establish but one disaster can destroy it. Let the journalist down once, give her a bum steer, forget to ring her back, tell her lies and you are finished not just with her but with her friends.

Credibility suffers when public relations begs. Genuine respect can only exist when there is professional confidence and competence on both sides. Public relations and journalism are just two professional jobs. Neither has any reason to be apologetic or deferential towards the other. But it is hard for the journalist to maintain respect for a public relations person who, despite several polite rebuttals, spends half the day phoning and begging for coverage of some person, event or product that is clearly not news. Or when she is carpet-bombed with press releases which are of no conceivable interest to anybody.

One side-effect of earned credibility is that when public relations has a problem and is desperate for coverage, the journalist friend will, all other things being equal, be prepared to help out. The news might be neither good, nor bad, just soft; not really earth-shattering, but important to the organisation that it be published. That cannot happen every day and certainly a dozen phonecalls, disturbing her when she is at her busiest, won't do the trick. Each helps when help is needed but there is no room for hypochondriacs.

Credibility is developed through understanding media realities, knowing the constraints and the deadlines to which journalists work and having an informed news sense.

Salinger's fourth and fifth points, making and maintaining personal contact, are linked to credibility. The journalist will be happier with the public relations person she knows. She will come to her as a trusted source. There will be sufficient understanding between them for information to be given off the record knowing that confidentiality will be respected. The journalist will believe that person.

It is important to keep in touch with the journalists whom one knows - don't allow the trail to go cold. One indication of having lost touch is the out-of-date mailing list. No amount of chummy 'Dear Leonie' and 'Best wishes, we must meet for lunch sometime' will overcome the scepticism of the journalist who receives mail sent to a paper which she left five years ago, or whose name is mis-spelt. One tip for good media relations is to have up-to-date mailing lists and to be fanatical about accuracy in spelling names and addresses.

It is a duty of public relations to be familiar with the media - that is with all newspapers, magazines, radio and television stations. Keep up-to-date with changes in personnel and in editorial policy. Read, listen, look to learn what sort of information is carried. If the woman's page was dropped two years ago, it is inexcusable today to send a story to the woman's editor. And don't send motoring news to a magazine which has never covered motor stories. The anonymously addressed 'agricultural correspondent' is a giveaway - one should know her name.

Does public relations always tell the truth, the whole truth and nothing but the truth ? No, and only the most naive journalist would expect it. What is told must be the truth, but there will always be a healthy tension between loyalty to employer and loyalty to the journalist as to how much one chooses to tell.

The advice of Bill Maxwell, former chief press officer for Aer Lingus, is never to ad lib with the media[3]. If not sure of the answer to a telephone query, say so, find out the facts and ring back. Journalists are experts at asking the question which gives the impression that they know more than they really do.

How much information is in the public interest ? Organisations are like families; not everything has to be revealed at all times. If one meets a friend in the street and she asks how things are at home, does one tell her literally everything ?

If an organisation wishes, it may choose not to comment, ever. That is bad public relations and bad business, but it is an organisation's right. But when something special happens who will then believe that organisation's 'no comment' or who will listen when there is good news which it wants the journalists to shout from the rooftops ? Journalists will be suspicious and feel they are being used.

Good media relations are tested especially in times of difficulty. Opening a new factory, creating 1000 new jobs, achieving a profit of £20 million against a loss of £5 million the previous year are all good news stories and it is easy to talk to the media about them.

But what if there is a factory closure, massive redundancies, heavy losses or scandal in the boardroom ? Is the organisation equally forthcoming then ? It should be, but frequently it is not.

The media are ephemeral. Today's newspaper wraps tomorrow's chips. Tonight's television news is superseded by some greater disaster tomorrow night. Good public relations means not sulking; it means accepting the rough with the smooth.

Sometimes the media get it all wrong. The journalist makes a mistake. The organisation is upset. But that very embarrassing story, or that terrible misquote, will most likely be forgotten tomorrow by almost every reader, and very few of them will have read it in the first place.

There is nothing wrong in bringing attention to a serious error. Respectable publications will apologise and probably publish a correction. But most of the time, if one feels misrepresented, forget it. The media have no time for whingers. Also, few write in praise when coverage has been good.

There is not a single organisation or institution in the country which believes its media coverage is always fair. Governments, churches, judges, trade unions, movie stars, singers, footballers always think the media have got it wrong. And sometimes they have.

Realise how much information has to be put together, checked and got out so quickly; it is amazing there are not more mistakes. The media can only be as accurate as is possible in the time available to prepare the story, and that could be as short as five minutes; they can seldom pretend to an accuracy that will stand the test of future historical research.

Media relations are an important part of public relations, but only a part. Journalists don't always realise this, so give them full attention. They think public relations is there solely to pester them, and in the early days of public relations that was the case, but some consultants now estimate that as little as 10 % of their time is spent on media relations. However, it still remains a very important channel for getting certain messages from an organisation to target audiences and for building up a good reputation.

16. News releases

EVERY day news releases are sent, often rushed by courier, from public relations departments and consultancies to newspapers, magazines and broadcasting stations. Comprising one or more typed (or, too often, hyped !) pages and often with photographs attached, they are presumed to be of interest to the publications concerned.

About 80 % are transferred straight from the news editor's desk to the wastepaper bin with barely a glance.

The news release is an over-used and badly-used tool. It should be sent only when it contains news, that is, fact or opinion that will be new and of interest to a substantial number of the publication's readers.

News has a mixture of four ingredients; it is new, relevant, of human interest and unusual.

It is new if the readers have not heard it before. Yesterday and to-day's events are new and newspapers strive to be ahead of one another in getting the most recent developments to their readers. When beaten by the evening television news, the morning papers have to get more up-to-date information. Round-the-clock satellite television is now making it more difficult for the newspapers to be first with the news; they are having to settle for more in-depth and informed commentary.

News is also relevant. If a car crashes in Buenos Aires, the reader in Dublin is unlikely to be interested. Much that happens in Buenos Aires, Calcutta, Tokyo and elsewhere goes unreported in Dublin. Relevance is what brings the news closer to home and enables the local reader to identify with it. If two Irish people were in the Buenos Aires crash it would probably get front page in the Dublin evening papers.

The tabloid papers over-emphasise the human interest side of news, but people are news and people doing things makes better news than people speaking. People identify with other people and want to read about them. Public figures make news easily, but are quickly forgotten once they go out of office. Royalty makes news in Britain because, while politicians come and go, the members of the royal family are on permanent display and are guaranteed news coverage to the end of their lives.

The unusual makes news. If a general election were held every day it would soon cease to be news but because it only comes every few years it can make and keep the front pages. Less earth-shattering events by eccentrics seeking entry to the *Guinness Book of Records* can make the front pages because they are unusual as well as being human.

News is like a cake. The ingredients are not mixed the same for every story, but a substantial proportion of them must be there. The daily newspaper or radio or television bulletin has a mixture of serious and less serious news.

Bad news grabs more attention than good news. This was always so, in heaven and on earth, for Christ asserted that there was more joy in heaven for the one sheep which strayed and came back than for the other ninety-nine.

Public relations must be objective about all information which is sent to the media and must not exaggerate its importance. It is news only if it will interest a substantial number of readers and if it is not news it must not be sent.

Look at how news is written for publication. The news story is short and snappy and starts with the most important information, moving through a series of short paragraphs from the more important to the less important details.

This is the inverted pyramid structure. The first two paragraphs - the intro - give the central information and answer the questions Who, Where, What, When, Why and How. The emphasis between the 5Ws and How will vary. For instance if the Taoiseach dies, 'Who' is the first question asked; if five people are killed in a boating tragedy, it is 'What' ; if the end of the world is about to be revealed, then most people will ask 'When'.

Those two paragraphs should be able to stand alone even if the rest of the story is cut away. The inverted pyramid allows the busy sub-editor, without re-writing, to reduce the story to any length she wishes by cutting paragraphs from the bottom up.

Get to the subject straight away. If attention is not grabbed in those first two paragraphs it will not be grabbed at all. The release cannot be a discursive essay, nor a detective story. There are but a few vital seconds to grab the news editor's attention and there is not a second chance.

It makes sense, then, for public relations to follow this style in news releases. But, no, many releases are long, boring and without news content. They are written more in hard-sell advertising than in journalistic language, with many empty adjectives and they go straight into the news editor's bin.

The news release is not a sales brochure. Its job is not to sell the product or the service to the journalist but to give her information which she can pass on to her readers because it will be of interest to them. If it is hard-sell the company would be better advised to take an advertisement.

Very often the news release is sent to the wrong journalist or wrong paper. If the knitting monthly does not have a motoring correspondent and has never covered motoring stories there is little point sending it a release about a new car.

Read the publications and know what sort of story they use. Be aware of deadlines and know them for each media outlet. Information is not going to be published if it arrives after deadline. Saturday night is not the time to send news for the Sunday paper; nor 31 March for the April edition of a monthly which is published on the first of every month.

News releases should not be scattered like confetti, but targeted and sent only to those who might be interested in them. It is not just the cost of another photocopy and a stamp to send it to another publication. The extra editor will wonder why it was sent and will doubt the professionalism of the sender and be conditioned to throw away anything else from the same source.

Junk mail in letterboxes is rarely read because it has not been targeted properly. Journalists receive many news releases and rarely have time to read them. If they know a particular person as a junk mail merchant they will be even less inclined to read her stuff. One sight of the letterhead will be enough to turn them off. On the other hand if one has built up respect and is seen to be professional they will stop, look and probably publish.

In one week the business editor of the London *Evening Standard* received 800 news releases and he used only two of them. He instanced one company which sent a release every morning and every afternoon. The stationery was distinctive and the envelope was never opened; just flung in the bin[4.]

Many people write bad releases, more to please the client than to achieve publication. They are full of advertising language, boastful and empty adjectives, sales talk, repetition of the company name, vacuous quotes from marketing managers and so on.

One spoof on the subject says: "Write your press releases in a style that appeals to the client rather than to a newspaper or magazine sub-editor. Tell the client that you are doing the exact opposite."[5] There might be some Machiavellian reason to that suggestion, but it is, of course, nonsense !

The news release most likely to be published will be on the news editor's desk in time, and in a form which enables her, if she wishes, to publish it without any change. And, it will be news, information that she is glad to receive, because it is interesting to her readers.

Write the release in the form of the inverted pyramid. Get the Who, Where, What, When, Why and How into the first two paragraphs and let the story flow from the most important to the least important details. Keep commercial jargon to a minimum, avoid sales talk. In describing company products and services, emphasise the uses and the advantages rather than the features. Personalise the story as much as possible.

Don't raise questions which are not answered. As the initiative has been taken in issuing the release, the information must be sufficiently complete not to leave unanswered questions for the reader.

Give the date at the top of the release and include name and telephone numbers, day and night, for further information.

At the end, supply further background information, specifications and company details for the editor.

The supply of information on discs means that old advice on the format of the news release will become less relevant, but, if written, the preferred practice is to type double-spaced on one side of the paper with generous margins. This is to allow the journalist to sub-edit and write instructions for the printer. The headed paper should identify the source but not be so designed as to take up half the page. The heading should bring the news editor's attention to the main point of the story.

Most news releases should fit on one page, or at the most, on two. If longer, read again and be prepared to trim. Remove the useless adjectives and the boastful references to the organisation. A release that is necessarily long because of complex and important information should contain a summary and highlights to facilitate rapid sub-editing. The announcement of a new appointment might be one sentence, if that is all a particular publication ever uses. But the same announcement going to a trade magazine might contain some biographical details about the person.

Even the best news release may not be published verbatim because every paper will have received it in the same form and each journalist will want to make it look as if it is her own. Ideally, the release should be so carefully targeted that it is re-written for each publication, highlighting an angle of special interest to that paper's readers. While time rarely allows this, different versions should be sent to each category of publication and certainly the broadcast media should receive a separate, usually briefer version with the spoken word in mind. A sports equipment magazine may take a more detailed description of a new tennis racket than the business page in a national daily. (Please don't send photographs to radio stations - it has happened !)

17.   Media events

MEDIA EVENTS include press briefings, photocalls, press conferences, press receptions and visits. They are held when a news release or phone-call is not sufficient and there is need for more detailed briefing with an opportunity for the media to meet the newsmakers or watch a demonstration.

The press briefing is a meeting with one or a few journalists, often over a drink or lunch. What is said is often off-the-record or for use without attribution. Journalists who specialise in areas like politics, industrial relations and business attend a lot of these briefings. Political correspondents, for instance, have daily, even twice daily briefings with the government press secretary.

The photocall is appropriate when photos only are needed. The art editor is the person to contact. An imaginative location can enhance this sort of story. Editors nowadays are more appreciative of good pictures and the commercial plug on page 16 can become the centre of page one if it comes with a good photograph. Be careful of backdrops because editors do not like photographs swamped by company names or gaudy logos.

The press conference is for important announcements, such as a company merger, or to explain a controversy, or put a rumour to rest, or reveal a major scoop like Hitler's diaries. The notice can be short because the news may be sudden and the emphasis is on the news rather than the social element. There is usually a top table with theatre-style seating. The host gives a statement and questions and answers follow. Copies of documents are circulated.

Do not annoy print journalists by pandering too much to

television crews, or delaying too long for them. The television people are often late and then take time to set themselves up. Remember that the print journalists have deadlines and have to get back to their offices.

Events such as US presidential press conferences are often shown live on television but they are carefully rehearsed, questions submitted in advance and the organisers adept at avoiding the difficult questioner or closing her down before she becomes an embarrassment.

Journalists who have weekly or monthly deadlines are sometimes reluctant to ask questions at press conferences lest they give away their special angles. They prefer to take the speaker aside afterwards.

The press reception tends to be a more social occasion, but it must be serious enough to be worth the journalists' time to attend. Many are questioning the cost-effectiveness of such occasions and they are now fewer than some years ago. Business executives and journalists have less time nowadays to stand around drinking and making small talk.

Softer news is usually kept for receptions. Who is there often gets more attention than what is announced.

Before arranging a press conference or reception be clear on the reasons for holding it. Plan everything in detail so that on the day it can look informal. Prepare speakers, with all likely questions rehearsed and scripts available.

Ensure that all equipment and visual aids have been tested beforehand. Rehearse everything, possibly the evening before, so that there will be time to put mistakes right. Don't arrive at the hotel just in time to meet the guests. Be there beforehand and check that everything is laid out as required. It is too late to find out five minutes before the event that due to a double booking the room has been changed and there are no blinds on the window.

Much time is spent checking and re-checking small details. Murphy's Law says that if anything can go wrong, it will go wrong. Public relations must learn O'Reilly's Law - that Murphy was an optimist !

From start to finish have a master and a daily checklist of

F

everything that must be done. It must be flexible and under constant revision. Confirm bookings, prices etc in writing.

Venues and times should be chosen to suit the journalists, not the organisation nor the guest speaker. City centre locations are favoured because most of the journalists have their offices there and can get out and back without losing too much time. Hotels are favoured because the good ones have the essential facilities on tap and are used to catering for such occasions.

Press conferences are usually held mid-morning or mid-afternoon, receptions in the early evening. If the main target is the evening paper or broadcast news, anything later than noon is useless; morning papers prefer mid-afternoon. Social events, held early evening, are geared primarily towards the columnists and, in Dublin, the diary columns in the following evening's papers. Don't make a habit of fixing times just to suit television, even though sometimes that may be desirable.

Never pick a day when big news is already anticipated. Nobody is able to compete with a general election, the budget, or an EC Summit Meeting in Dublin.

Tuesday, Wednesday and Thursday are bad when Dail, Seanad and courts are sitting. Friday and Saturday are bad for the business pages. Bank holidays are usually avoided, but some now find that Sunday afternoons are good. It is easier to get news space on a Monday morning and the evening columnists also need material for Monday.

Journalists should be invited in writing between three and ten days in advance. Sooner than that and the invitation may be lost. If sent to the news editor it will be entered in the diary for attention on the day.

The invitation indicates what is happening without giving the whole story away. It is addressed to the news editor and/or the specialist journalist who might have an interest in the event. It is not sent only to that journalist, because she might be away. There is always a news editor on duty.

Invitations should be followed by a phonecall to confirm they have been received. It can help to offer transport to and from the event if the venue is out of town. Attendance cannot be promised at this stage as newsrooms only decide coverage on the day. The RSVP tag is never taken seriously. Irish media are especially perverse about this; something which the British find hard to understand.

Target a few key journalists whose attendance is desired more than the rest and concentrate follow-up on them. Explain the story in greater detail to them. In fact, consult them before deciding to hold the event lest it clash with something else. Don't arrange a reception for the motoring journalists without checking whether they might be in South America that week test-driving a new Japanese car.

The press conference is only for the media, never mix sales people. There is more flexibility at a press reception, particularly to keep up the numbers, but never make the presentations a sales pitch. A reception for journalists only is embarrassing if none of them turns up.

What would otherwise be a soft news event can be enhanced by the presence of a celebrity. This can be good at product launches. Pick the celebrity carefully. Some of them are dear and very precious and they are useless if not available to talk to journalists and give interviews. Don't overestimate the importance of broadcasters, particularly those who have just "arrived". Why should experienced print journalists be impressed by these people who are not yet their peers?

Press material should be distributed on arrival. Don't overdo it. Success does not demand a presskit in a cardboard folder. The single news release might be adequate, but if it is felt that other material needs to be included, then go ahead. It could be background notes, speeches, brochures, biographical details and photographs if they have been taken in advance.

Irish journalists do not favour name tags on their lapels. However, the executives of the host organisation should be clearly identified.

Some organisations give gifts to journalists at receptions. They should be small and relevant. Food and book launches lend themselves to samples and free copies, but forget about microwave ovens, radios, videos and free travel tickets.

Always have one's own photographer. She should be an NUJ member and briefed beforehand. Her first function is to take photographs and supply them to deadline for those in attendance who have not brought their own photographer. National papers will usually have their own photographer or not use a photograph at all, but magazines appreciate this service.

Refreshments are a secondary consideration at a press conference. Coffee and biscuits might be adequate, depending on time of day. A non-routine press briefing in mid-day, however, might merit a lunch for those who have time to stay. These refreshments are served after the main business has been completed.

The press reception and the arranged visit to the organisation lend themselves to greater hospitality. Customs vary but the tendency is to press a drink into the visitor's hand straight away, as one would if she visited one's home. Remember that the journalist who drinks and talks most is often marginal. The top journalists usually have to hurry off quickly.

The press reception in a good hotel with drinks, sandwiches and savouries costs an average of £10 per head. Care should be taken with all food, drink and entertainment, unless the budget is open-ended. Estimates should be got from the hotel beforehand.

Agree on a time or an amount for closure and tell the barman. Be careful when the official business is over and everybody is chatting merrily beside an open bar. If the client wants to extend the bar make sure she signs for it. Otherwise when the bill is presented she will conveniently forget that she authorised the extension.

Media events tend to start late. The press conference should be more prompt, even if one's favourite journalist is not there. The reception allows more flexibility, but if nothing has happened by 6 o'clock for a 5.30 reception, it is discourteous.

Press material is sent immediately after the reception to the national daily newsrooms who were not represented and they are phoned to see if they would like photographs. All publications must be monitored for coverage, but never complain about those who attended and did not publish anything. One cannot buy coverage merely by throwing a lavish reception. No matter how good the reception, if the story is not strong enough, or if some other big news happens, one can lose out.

18.   Speechwriting

PEOPLE in public relations may write hundreds, even thousands of speeches over a lifetime, varying in length from one page to twenty, from two minutes to half an hour or more.

Speeches are written for presidents, taoisigh, government ministers, county councillors, chairmen, chief executives, marketing managers and anybody else who has to say a few words. On some occasions there might be several weeks to prepare, on others, ten minutes or less !

Speechwriting is a chore for some. They know that few listen to speeches and even fewer remember them. But, whether it be the opening of a new bridge, or an exhibition or the launching of a new product, the few words have to be said. Somebody has to write them knowing they may be delivered in a monotone incantation and that everybody will applaud politely, trying to balance their drink in one hand while clapping with the other two !

It is very boring to listen to a reading speaker who is unaware of her next page. One government minister had a valued and trusted speechwriter and he never checked ahead what had been written for him. But he was the sort of man who on first reading could make the script sound as if he meant every word of it. His scriptwriter was retiring and as a last gesture to his minister and friend he let the speech run in its usual impeccable style until the minister turned over to page five where he read: "Thanks for everything, X. I shall miss you. You are on your own now" - followed by blank pages.

Speeches need not be chores. They can be golden opportunities which cost little and deliver important messages. There is also the possible spin-off to a wider audience through media coverage.

The alert executive seeks opportunities for speakers to deliver messages for the organisation. Many professional and voluntary bodies which organise lunches, seminars and other meetings welcome suggestions for speakers - but they must be good and have something relevant to say.

Not all platforms are suitable. Certain radio and television programmes might not suit certain company messages; likewise platforms. Public relations has to be alert and advise accordingly. Few would advise the Taoiseach to choose *Nighthawks* as the programme for his analysis of the economy; ironically, however, it was on *Nighthawks*, in January 1992, that former Justice minister, Sean Doherty, gave the short interview which led to the resignation of Charles Haughey[6].

Check in advance what publicity plans the organisers have and back them up. Not the whole speech, but a highlight of the important points, the desired message with a news angle, may be circulated to the media.

The speech might seem to be over in 20 minutes but publicity can make it last a lifetime.

Public speaking frightens most people and all good plans come to nothing if the speaker is not prepared or trained. If the chief executive is a poor speaker and has not improved with training and experience some other executive should be picked out.

Former British Conservative MP, Robert S.Redmond, has said it is time for organisations providing lecturers for seminars and presentations to think of the "appalling PR effect of monotonous, inaudible muttering". He adds that there is such a difference between the spoken and written words and "such a pity that so few - even learned academics - realise it"[7].

Many of the best speakers look as if they are casual and off-the-cuff, but they are not. Winston Churchill, famous for his speaking and his ad lib witticisms, practiced one hour on average for every minute of his speeches. He rehearsed, polished and tested his phrases for likely effect. Businessman Tony O'Reilly, excellent on the conference and after-dinner circuit and the late John Kelly, minister and TD, famed for his rasping contributions to Dail debates, have been meticulous in their preparation.

In writing the speech, the brief is important. Find out what the speaker would like to say, her views and feelings towards the occasion and its significance. Read other recent speeches which she has made and get background information about the occasion on which she will be speaking.

The speaker may not brief the speechwriter. She may just say; "give me a quarter of an hour. You know the sort of things I like to say".

That can be fine if speaker and speechwriter know each other well, but the two might never meet, for public relations often sub-contracts speech-writing to specialists. The fees for the top people can be high. It could be up to £500 in Ireland for a 15-minute speech, with lesser amounts for shorter ones. In the US the top writers can get between $5,000 and $7,000 dollars a speech; good money, but put into perspective when one considers what celebrities can get for delivering those words - Ronald Reagan charged $2 million dollars for a four-minute speech in Japan.

In writing, be conscious of the audience. Don't aim too high or too low. A meeting of cub scouts will not appreciate a detailed analysis of the American economy, nor will an international gathering of nuclear scientists need an idiot's guide to how electricity was invented. The late Bishop Lucey of Cork, though, delivered his most erudite and critical utterances at confirmation ceremonies.

As with any other form of writing it is best to think for a while, getting thoughts into some sort of order, and then, just let it fly. The first draft won't be perfect but once the words are on paper there is a product to work on.

Don't try to say too much. The audience have limited ability to absorb and retain. Unlike the pages of a book which they can turn back, they hear the speech once, so it cannot be too cluttered and it must flow logically. Also, give examples which are meaningful and relevant to them.

First, there should not be too many ideas in a speech, nor uneven jumps from one topic to another. The ideas should be logically developed with smooth transitions. Learn from the technique of the *What it Says in the Papers* programme on RTE Radio. Listeners have to be eased from one idea to the next.

Model frameworks can be suggested for preparation of speeches, but they have to be flexible. For instance, if the organisation is embarking on a new business strategy, the speaker can move through "where we were, to where we are and where we're going". Or, for the introduction of a new product or service, her line can be from "what it is and how it works, who benefits from it and why the audience should care about it".

There must be room for pause, repetition to reinforce a point, asides for lighter comment. The speech is not an essay nor an analysis and it must not be written as such. Keep it conversational and be careful with figures and statistics. If the organisation's net profit for the year was £15,365,000, it might be better in delivery to just say "more than £15 million".

Some advise first to tell the audience what one is going to say, then say it, then tell them what one has said. Yes, but not too literally, except in a longer speech. There should be flexibility to allow for the surprise element.

If one wants to make a very strong point, it is good to lead up to it and to reiterate it. possibly with further homely examples. It can be easily lost through a momentary distraction if it is passed over too quickly.

Be careful with humour. It has to suit the audience. If the writer has never met the speaker, it is hard to gauge her sense of humour. More speakers fail than succeed with their attempts at humour. Avoid long-winded jokes and be in good taste, conscious of the audience.

The opening must be strong to grab audience attention. It may be best to write these paragraphs last, but they should be chiselled and worked upon until they are perfect.

Likewise the ending. There should be a rounded-off feeling. The speech cannot end abruptly like the news story in inverted pyramid form. The listeners have to feel they are going away with something. A strong finish, a call to action, the spontaneous raising of the fist in the air. That is what will get the standing ovation !

And, finally, advise the speaker, if possible, to read without the script. Not always possible, and certainly not for government ministers who might make several speeches in the one day, but it is the ideal. Many speeches are ruined by overdependence on notes or scripts and visual aids. If there has to be a script, type it in upper and lower case, not in capitals. Upper and lower case script is read 13.4 times as rapidly as capitals - therefore, in any context, capitals are harder to read.

19. Newsletters

ORGANISATIONS have been publishing newsletters since long before the recognition of public relations as a management function. They became common in the mid-19th century.

Newsletters appear at regular intervals, rather than once-off brochures. They are mostly tabloid like newspapers, A4 like magazines, or A5 like books. Tabloid is best when most of the stories are short and newsy with plenty of photographs; A4 if the tendency is for longer articles and A5 for research papers and analytical material.

Internal newsletters are for employees and externals for outside audiences. Some attempt to be both but they have to lean towards the external as outside audiences are not interested in trivial personal details and sports and social events.

Organisations often underestimate the importance of their newsletters and adopt an unprofessional approach. Many deserve the description given by Robert Townsend, former Chairman of Avis in his book, *Up the Organisation*, where he said that reading them was like going down for the third time in lukewarm treacle.

"Many in-house publications are launched to boost egos, and continue because no-one has bothered to find out if they are still relevant", says British business writer, Andrew Crofts. "Consequently, they are a waste of time and money. They are produced by over-cautious people, and rendered unreadable by nit-pickers"[8].

For British consultant, Steve Nickolls, many organisations fail to exploit the opportunity provided by newsletters and this is mainly because they fail to recognise "the three Rs found in every successful journal; it must be respected, readable and regular".[9]

Hundreds of Irish organisations have newsletters but nobody has researched them. In the UK, there are an estimated 3,000 publications with more than 15 million readers a month and expenditure of about £33 million. In the US, there are at least 100,000 publications, with a probable turnover of $1 billion, but this includes the vast industry of special interest newsletters which are published commercially and taken by subscription.

Questions should be answered before a new newsletter is

published. Is it needed ? Could the same message reach its audience through a staff meeting, press release or brochure. Not every organisation has sufficient news to merit a regular newsletter and it shows after the enthusiasm of the first issue, lessening off by the second and probably disappearing after the third with loss of credibility and waste of money.

What is its purpose ? If it is merely to imitate other similar organisations, or because the chief executive feels there should be one, that is not enough. It should only be published to meet a definite need to communicate. Most large organisations need newsletters, especially when staff are dispersed over several locations or when there has been a history of poor internal communication. External newsletters respond to an outside audience needing greater awareness of the organisation and to remove misunderstanding after some policy decision or activity. But there must be something to say on a regular basis.

Who are the audience ? Internally, is it for management or for production staff or for everybody ? Externally, has the market been defined ?

How regular ? To be respected, the publication must come out on time. If monthly and published on the 10th of the month, then it must appear every 10th.

What do the readers want ? The Americans asked them and a survey in 1990, in co-operation with *Industry Week* magazine, found chief executives to be most concerned with the following issues: product quality, cutting labour or production costs, the organisation's future, keeping up with technology, product development, compliance with regulations, product liability, environmental control, competition from imports, employees' drug use. Employees wanted information about the organisation's future, the competition, reasons for important decisions and actions, corporate goals and direction, opportunities for career advancement, product development, employee benefits, the corporate strength and stability, product quality and quality improvement efforts, financial results.

It was found that of every 100 articles published in employee print media, only 25 were focused on any one of the topics highlighted by chief executives; only five were about their most important concern, product quality; and only seven covered the topic of most interest to employees, the company's future. Less than one in 200 publications featured letters to the editor, a question and answer column, or an open forum.

The most common form of publication was two or four page, magazine A4 format, monthly or bi-monthly. Topics most favoured by editors were personal news and employee recreation.[10]

Internal newsletters lose the respect of their readers if they are merely management mouthpieces. They should allow an exchange of ideas, two-way communication.

That does not mean that the editor should expect a free hand to create controversy as in a private commercial publication. The newsletter should not be used in disputes between management and employees and it is questionable if it is suitable for responding to outside criticism. Newsletters are accused of being too safe, but one has to consider the chief executive and the many audiences whom she has to satisfy at the one time. She gains nothing by knocking any of them.

The external newsletter descends to propaganda and loses respect through telling only the good things and boasting repeatedly about the achievements of its staff. Every picture is of a smiling chief executive or award-winner or benefactor. There seem to be no problems. The mature organisation should get beyond this and write in a more balanced way about itself, as when, after a rail crash in London, the most searching analysis and the stiffest interview with the chief executive of British Rail appeared in the company's own newspaper for staff.

Who should be the editor ? It does not matter what title she has nor what department she works within, as long as she has both journalistic and public relations skills, and preferably marketing awareness also. She has to absorb the culture of the organisation and that is difficult, but not impossible, for the consultant or outside publisher. The public relations manager or consultant is the obvious person to be editor, but surprisingly many organisations leave it to the personnel department and often to a junior person who has neither journalistic nor public relations experience.

The chief executive should appoint an editor in whom she has confidence and then let her get on with the job. It is better not to burden her with an editorial committee. Nor should material have to be cleared through line management. The only clearance should be by the editor through the chief executive in whose name it is published.

The production should be high quality in every respect. That is why a good professional is needed - to write properly, to design, to layout, to use photographs and give readers the feeling that it is as good, if not better, than commercial newspapers or magazines.

Appearance is important because most newsletters are read rapidly, or merely glanced at. Professional design does much to show that the organisation is serious and cares, but beware, sometimes, of outside designers; they are not necessarily best, because they are often non-journalists and are preoccupied with appearance rather than content.

Poor publications are an insult to staff. "Stale internal communications pile up like dandruff on a company's sense of self", says Tim Aston, a UK designer. "The message which an indifferent communication sends out to staff is just that: indifference".[11] Advances in desk top publishing have meant there is no excuse for not having a professional-looking newsletter. But, the technology cannot be better than the person using it. The wonders of DTP do not dispense from the need to be professional and experienced in typography and design.

Circulation can be a major cost. Even for staff, the ideal would be to post it home to everybody. Most organisations take the easier way out and leave it around the workplace or in communal areas, where it often remains unread and untouched.

For the external newsletter there must be a targeted and accurate mailing list which is kept up to date. News media may be included, as some news from the organisation is picked up in this way, having been ignored when previously circulated through press release.

Should staff pay for the newsletter ? A nominal sum, given to charity might create more respect for it, but collection is a further administrative chore and it should be weighed up against the benefits.

This also applies to advertising. Publications for big corporations can attract advertisers because they reach many people, but is it worth the administrative effort and is the newsletter seen to have failed if advertising is not maintained ?

The printed newsletter has been familiar for 150 years. But this could be changing. Some corporations have their own satellites and Texas Instruments, in Dallas, for instance, use an electronic newspaper to communicate daily with most of their 70,000 staff worldwide and these staff can access news on their personal computers via the company communication system. That may be the style of the future, but the printed paper product will always have the flexibility that it can be brought anywhere, read anywhere and passed around, without the help of any electronic gadget. Some people will always prefer it that way.

20. Brochures

BROCHURES are in many shapes and sizes; from expensive, glossy booklets to smaller, throwaway sales leaflets. They give a corporate or product message to a target audience. The reasons for the brochure decide which form is most appropriate.

When asked to produce a brochure, be clear what is needed. Have a definite brief before approaching writers, designers, photographers or printers.

There are many reasons why organisations need, or at least want, new brochures. The long-established and well-known organisation wants to tell its history; the department store, to let customers know about its products and special offers; the company which is going public, or expects to be the target of a takeover bid, to give information about itself to the financial community; universities and schools, to inform prospective students about their courses, or to attract research grants and sponsorship; tour operators, to get holiday-makers to book now for their sun-filled attractions; charities, to attract further aid; the Industrial Development Authority, to get overseas industrialists to invest in Ireland.

Vanity is not a sufficient reason for a brochure; nor is imitation of competitors.

Some brochures just tell a story, others help sell a product or a service. Most of them try to do a bit of both. Be clear beforehand which is the dominant purpose - to tell or to sell.

Before talking to writers, designers, photographers or printers, decide on the purpose, the budget, the readership and the expected shelf-life of the publication. Fashions change, executives move, a brochure can become obsolete very easily. It is pointless printing 5000 if only 500 are really needed The unit cost for 500 might seem higher, but it is better than eventually having to dump 4500.

Who handles brochure production ? It is normally public relations, but advertising agencies also have some expertise. As with newsletters, the advertising people are probably better if the hard sell is required - they are used to punchy copywriting and grabbing layouts. But, if the primary purpose is to tell - company history, financial details, employee information - then, the hype of advertising is unconvincing and the better choice is public relations.

Content is the core of the brochure. That is the message. Design and production decisions reinforce it and help to get it across. The writer should liaise with designer, photographer and printer.

Ideally, a rough design is planned before the copy is written. Avoid having too much copy. Readers don't like a cluttered appearance or large chunks of type, but prefer it broken up with graphics, photographs and varied design.

The A4-size page, in its upright (tall) form rather than landscape (broad), is better for an information brochure because it is easier to file. Large sizes and odd shapes may be attention-grabbing but are less suitable. Sales brochures can be in any size or shape with all sorts of windows, unusual folds and anything else which makes an impact.

"A designer in the field of special publications becomes as much inventor of folds and cuts as manipulator of type and art", says Roy Paul Nelson, Professor of Journalism, University of Oregon, USA, pointing to the originality in design and production that has been made possible by advances in print technology. [12]

It is a skill of public relations to write the copy but design is best left to the specialist. In picking a designer it is horses for courses. Some are dull and unimaginative. They perform on time and to budget, but without great flair. There is a sameness about their work. Others are more creative and original, but often disorganised with panic and alarms as deadline approaches. Do not necessarily take the easier option. It can be worth the extra stress to go for the creative one.

Remain in control. The designer might like an idea but it does not have to be accepted. She can run riot with budgets, producing marvellous but expensive work, if she is allowed. Printers used do the typesetting; now the designer looks after it. Let her suggest typefaces and typesizes but do not let fancy design reduce readability. The comfort of the reader must come first. Remember, for instance, that it can be difficult to read type on coloured backgrounds and almost impossible to read white type against light colour.

The first design stage is the rough, a pencilled sketch with a general idea of style and size. This is followed by a dummy of the complete brochure with same paper and binding and number of pages to give a feel of the finished job. Next comes a full mock-up with real or dummy photographs and the text stripped in in gibberish Latin but showing the final typefaces, backgrounds, colour etc. Then, there is finished art work, ready for the printer.

As in so many other areas, these traditional methods are being revolutionised and computer-generated designs can do in seconds what formerly took hours of back-breaking labour.

If doing the brochure for a client, get her to sign the finished artwork because there will not be any changes after that. If the client has not approved, one can be liable for the re-print cost if there is an error.

Photography is integral to the publication and worth doing properly. It can be expensive, up to £500 a day, but it is better, and insignificant compared to the printing costs in a major job. Be careful in taking photographs from old files; they lack the freshness of new ones and such features as dress or cars might show them to be dated. Photographs should be taken with knowledge of the design. As most brochures are now in colour, transparencies are better than glossy prints.

Finally, the printer is given camera-ready art work which is then converted to a plate and mounted on the print machine.

Always get quotations from a few printers because prices vary greatly, even with the same firm from one job to another. There is a lot of capacity in the print industry and firms are hungry for business.

Know the printing firm. Be aware of its capacity and see examples of similar work which it has done. The small printer who specialises in letterheads and invoice sheets is not necessarily the best for a big multi-colour job. Deadlines can be a problem. Printers will always look for more time than they need, as protection against machines breaking down, operators going sick, or a more prestigious job coming in and having to be finished in a hurry. But, if the money is right printers perform miracles.

Like the newsletter, the brochure can be a very effective way to communicate and it can have a long life, but it must have a purpose, a message and an identified audience.

21.　Annual Reports

THE ANNUAL REPORT is the shareholders' main single source of information about their organisation. It is valuable also for employees, financial analysts, bankers and journalists. Positive investment decisions are influenced not only by good performance but by communication through such exercises as the annual report.

Financial regulations do not require the glossy report that is now the practice in most organisations, but they give this further information because of the importance audiences who will read it. The idea of the brochure-type report is not new. As far back as 1957 a writer in *The Scotsman* said: "There is now a growing tendency to publish reports and accounts for a wider readership than shareholders. The annual report has become a vehicle of publicity and of management-employee relationships"[13]. British food group, Allied-Lyons, print 30,000 copies more than their share register requires.

"The bigger, better annual report has become for the corporate centre what the major trade fair often is for the operating company: a party that it cannot afford not to be seen at", says publisher Eileen Scholes[14].

Private companies are not required to publish full accounts but with EC law requiring more disclosure, some of them are doing so voluntarily, being proud of their achievements and having nothing to hide. Superquinn gave the lead among Irish supermarket chains but when their competitors did not follow suit, they dropped the idea.

The earliest surviving annual report is the minute book for the Company of Painters and Stainers in York, dated 1510. Leather-bound and well-designed, it contains a full account of receipts and payments.

"Researchers tell us that the private shareholder spends on average just one minute looking at an annual report", says John Cole, consultant in financial public relations. "Considering the time and effort put in, it is perhaps one of the few documents that is read more before it is published than afterwards"[15].

The American estimate is an average cost of $4 for each copy of an annual report. *The Times* has suggested a medium-sized UK company is now prepared to spend £3 to £4 a copy compared to £1 in the early 1980s. Communications conglomerate WPP spent £15 a copy for a report that was a boxed set of two volumes. Postage often costs even more than production.

The Trustee Savings Bank Group in the UK say their report costs £1.8 million and many individual investors do not read it. They want a change in law to allow a simpler report for small investors which would lay out in straightforward and readable terms how the company is performing.

Colm Rapple, *Evening Press* business editor, defines the annual report as "a report in words and figures on the performance or current state of an enterprise"[16]. He points out that it is not necessarily an objective document, as all sorts of accounts can be produced from one set of facts without falsifying the reality.

The most commonly published report is the standard profit and loss accounts for shareholders, which is statutorily required of public companies and state bodies. But other forms of report can be

G

produced for other audiences. Banks like cash flow accounts which describe flow of cash rather than profits. Tax accounts are prepared to show tax liability and highlight factors which reduce profits. Economists like value-added accounts which are directed at a broader public and show how much of the wealth created by the company has gone to workers, the state, banks etc.

The heart of the report is the audited financial statement showing the balance sheet, profit and loss account, source and application of funds, notes to the accounts and the auditor's report. It should be well presented in readable typefaces allowing easy comparison with the previous year.

Annual reports can be difficult for non-specialists to read but they are examined in minute detail by analysts and accountants. The layman, for instance, might skim over the notes to the accounts but that is where the most important information may be revealed.

The balance sheet can be particularly confusing. It is merely a snapshot of the company at year end, detailing assets and liabilities on a given date. It has nothing to do with performance.

The report must also include a directors' statement with information about major changes in the company. This gives an overview of the year's activities, with reference to profit and loss account, dividends, information on directors and their shareholdings.

The chairman's statement is probably read first by the layman but, to the expert, it is the least important item. It is not part of the statutory requirement and it is frequently used to comment on performance in a bland, subjective way, playing down the embarrassments and accentuating the positive. It is good public relations to put the bad news up front in this statement.

The report comes to shareholders three weeks before the annual general meeting and contains other documentation relating to the meeting - official notice, agenda,the proxy voting-card. These are usually incorporated in the main document with a perforated edge for tearing off.

Most good annual reports have a central unifying theme - a clear editorial message. It could be growth, new acquisitions, stability, international expansion, recovery. The theme will originate from the company's most pressing messages. It will run through the text, the illustrations and the design. There is plenty of scope for thematic development, for a report of 60 pages might have only 16 that are strictly speaking part of the audited accounts and statutory requirement.

"Themed reports get better readership, no matter what industry they represent. If the annual report has a strong theme that tells an exciting story about what the company is doing, or where it is going, it will be read", says New York designer, John Waters.[17]

Aer Rianta, the Irish airports authority, in its annual report for 1988, emphasised the theme of so much being new in the company - new duty free shops, new buildings, new runway, unprecedented growth and expansion. This was reflected throughout in the chairman's statement, the management review, the photographs, the graphics. Quotes were highlighted: "We spent more on airport development than ever before"; "New records were again established for passenger throughput";".....strong performance of the UK and European sectors"; "Employee relations continued to be excellent", and so on.

It is desirable that a senior executive, preferably the manager of public relations, be responsible for the annual report, but she must have time to devote to it as well as the authority to take decisions. She is not on her own but is one of a team which can include chief executive, department heads, accountants, writers, designers and others. The production schedule will extend over most of the year.

Journalist Jeremy Myerson, says: "Even the best designed document can be crushed to death by stilted language that generates boredom and disbelief rather than conviction in the company's strengths. So while design must be used to create a good first impression, the words need crafting to ensure the message gets through". He adds that in a way the design should be something one does not notice. "It is clean and balanced and drives the text forward"[18].

Concern that the ordinary shareholder and the staff do not read the report has led, particularly in the US, to a series of gimmicks, and even in the UK there have been examples of pop-up productions. In the US, Allied Supermarkets put its report in a brown paper bag;

Warner Communications went punk, with purple tints on the chairman's picture; spice maker MacCormick impregnated its report with its special flavours and office furniture manufacturer Herman Miller published a photograph, 1.5 inches high of each of its 3265 employees.

Mere gloss does not impress the serious investor. In this sense the annual report is different from most other publications. If the figures are not right, no amount of cosmetics will impress.

There is no flexibility with printers' deadlines. The shareholders, by law, have to receive the printed report within the required period before the meeting. There may be delays in final approval of the accounts, so that the time for printing might be very short. This can cause complications with large, glossy-coloured productions.

"If the job falls to you to prepare a company's next annual report, remember a few basic rules : plan carefully, combine informative financial statements with clarity, use compelling visual elements - and do it with style", John Cole[19].

22.   Photographs

PICTURE editors complain about poor photographs from public relations people. "…. I cannot fail to be amazed and horrified at the standard of photographs supplied by public relations companies", says Alun John, former picture editor of *The Independent*. "I feel insulted by them. In many cases they are rubbish"[20].

The good photograph says even more than a thousand words about an organisation, product or service. It is invaluable. Witness the impact of a photograph dominating page one of a daily newspaper. If that relates to a product or activity, surely there is no comparison in impact with a news release which has been gutted and locked away on page 16. Politicians realise the importance of the photo-opportunity and are prepared to submit to the most ridiculous stunts. Indeed, election campaigns are no longer speaking tours but series of planned photo-opportunities with occasional 'bytes' for radio and television.

Newspapers' increased use of good photographs is a result of improved print technology and familiarity with television and its emphasis on the visual.

Events can be arranged with photo-opportunities in mind. A scenic location is more attractive than a dull factory or a meeting room. During the Irish European Presidency in 1990, meetings were set up at Dromoland and Ashford castles, in addition to Dublin Castle and the other familiar locations, very much with photo-opportunities in mind.

Photographers like to work outside unless it is raining, so bear this in mind and accommodate them as much as possible.

There does not have to be a press conference or a major announcement. If there is a good picture possibility, have a photocall. Be inventive with angles and locations. A musical company publicised its Dublin production with a photocall at the Forty Foot, a traditional male bathing spot. The dancing girls in swimsuits contrasted so humorously with naked male flesh that they made the front news pages of the morning papers.

Newspapers prefer to take their own pictures, with no words visible nor any hint of advertising. Therefore, avoid company logos and backdrops. The client, however, might have opposite values. She wants her people to send out "puff" pictures (especially of two people shaking hands across a cheque), making sure the product name shouts out. The client must be educated to reality.

Always have one's own photographer and if the press don't attend, send in pictures, properly captioned, as quickly as the papers need them - within two hours.

Newspaper layouts now favour one good photograph to dominate each page. But it must have something special - the unusual, the personal, people doing something rather than staring at the camera. Some years ago, British politician Ken Livingstone was news every time he went out of his home. "Red Ken" he was called and the incongruity of his picture in *The Guardian* wearing six hats and smiling, stopped the reader in his tracks. The clever caption completed the impact: "Hat trick....Ken Livingstone let things go to his head when he stood in as model yesterday, previewing next week's show at Olympia to heighten the dress sense of the British male"[21].

Avoid what is disparagingly called the 'PR photograph'. That can be the firing-squad shot of a group of bored business people staring at the camera, holding their tummies in and doing nothing, but dwarfed in front of a large company logo and banner. Or it can be a grin-and-grab shot of a smiling young person receiving a cheque or cup from an equally smiling business mogul with a third, or even fourth smiling executive also squeezing into the picture.

Philip N. Douglis, US consultant, says: "If there is a typical organisational photo-cliché for the late 20th century, it has to be a shot such as this one: somebody, with phone to ear, looks at computer and types on keyboard".

He adds: "The best way to photographically treat any subject is to not just describe it by offering an illustration but instead to interpret it, creating communications"[22].

Preferably there should be no more than three or four people in a group photograph - one is ideal if he is doing something sufficiently interesting or is in a pose which tells a story. Photographs can be very candid and they easily pick up body language - a worried chairman adjusting his tie on his way into the annual meeting, the bored member of the audience and so on.

If the photograph is posed keep it narrow and have the people close together, even touching shoulders. Also, three people in a photo do not have to be side by side. Their positioning can be a statement on their hierarchical ranking. They can be one behind the other, or one sitting and two standing; the photographer can stand on a table and look down at them - numerous possibilities.

When photographing a product, come close enough to see the details, especially any new or important features. Somebody using the product (not a female model draped over it) makes a better picture than the product standing on its own.

Humorous pictures are remembered by readers long after all of the others - therefore, if humour gets your serious message across, use it. "Institutions tend to fear humour because it is reality, and such reality is too honest, hits too close to home", writes Philip N. Douglis.[23] Photographs should always be submitted with captions attached firmly , but never stapled. Nor should one write on the back of the photograph. The caption should live on its own and have the same identifying details as the news release which may or may not accompany it. Some news releases are merely extended captions.

The caption must identify clearly who is in the picture, from left to right, and say what is happening. But it can be written in punchy style to suit the mood of the photograph. The reader should be impelled from looking at the picture to reading the caption.

To ensure accuracy have somebody assist the photographer with captions, taking names, titles and spellings; from left to right. There is one organisation which features social pictures in its newsletter, but one rarely sees all of the people identified in correct position with correct spelling.

Target pictures carefully and only send if there is a reasonable chance of publication. Do not send the same photograph to more than one paper.

It is surprising how often people send out photos and invite to photocalls without checking what the papers want. Offer a real exclusive and they will jump to the suggestion. But, take trouble to find out what they want. Study their publications. Know their preferences and their deadlines.

Some magazines want colour work several weeks in advance; television wants all visuals and graphics early in the day, to have any hope for the evening news. *The Irish Times* say all photo chances are dead after 7 p.m, *The Irish Press* and *The Irish Independent* would go a bit earlier. That does not mean a bomb exploding in the city at 10 pm is ignored, but that the non-staff photograph will get no attention if it is late. Noon is probably the latest for a Dublin evening paper.

When engaging a photographer, brief her properly. If one does not know what one wants she will just do the job quickly, snapping groups of happy people in grin-and-grab and firing squad formations. She will do that, not because she is a bad photographer, but because it is what most of her clients want her to do. But if she sees that good photography is expected and appreciated, she will respond.

"Photographers are imaginative people, but they're also human", says Mark Warner, a British press photographer. "If all you ask for is a handshake shot, then it's easy to shoot and less time consuming. But if you show enthusiasm for producing a bright picture - and above all give him or her some time and co-operation, then you may discover that your usual PR photographer has hitherto hidden talents"[24].

Photographers for press work should have experience in the field and be NUJ members. The good commercial photographer, used to taking weddings and insurance shots of accident victims, may not have the awareness and the contacts for press work. She certainly will not appreciate nor want to work to the deadlines of the newspapers.

Photographers like to have some time before the event to check out their locations and backgrounds. They have needle eyes for background details, such as peeling wallpaper, the missing button or the unwanted shaft of light.

"If you read a daily newspaper or have magazines around the house, you already have some of the best photographic textbooks available. Study the pictures used. Try to figure out why a picture grabs and holds your attention. Is it because it is of a famous personality ? Is it the composition of the picture ? Is it the expression of someone's face ? Is it the action ?", writes Dorothy I. Doty, New York public relations consultant[25].

23.   Television & Video

EASIER access to improved, cheaper technology has made television and video an exciting modern tool for public relations. But, it must be a case of 'look before you leap'. Why is it wanted ? What is it going to do that could not be done better by some other means ? Is it the best way to get across the corporate message ?

If one decides to use it, one must be prepared to spend enough money to use it properly. Staff, customers and the general public expect the same professional standards from corporate productions as from professional television channels.

"For corporate videos to work, holding their audience's interest, they must adhere to the same courtesies and conventions as those for TV programming. The audiences for videos may be captive, but that does not prevent them becoming bored or uninterested if the product is not up to the mark", says film producer, Louis Marcus[26].

In business the advantages of video were first recognised for training, as the successor to the film strip. Comedian John Cleese made his money not so much for his role in *Fawlty Towers* as for his production of training videos, using his inimitable style of humour. Now there is also an emphasis on employee communications, environmental issues and financial services, as well as corporate propaganda.

The principal use in public relations for TV and video has been the corporate production, basically an electronic brochure and having a lifetime of a few years. There is now, in addition, a growing use of the video news release (VNR) and the company-produced TV programme which is sent over a private satellite network.

Corporate video production is a booming business in Ireland, with many companies reaching high professional standards. Some broadcasters are partners in these companies, lending their reputation and credibility - Gay Byrne, Mike Murphy and Pat Kenny, for instance.

The International Industrial Film and Video Congress, in Dublin in 1988, was a major boost for the industry in Ireland, increasing business awareness of it. The Confederation of Irish Industry (CII) give a prize for the best Irish entry in this annual event.

The CII perceives video not only as essential for marketing communication, but also as an industry very suited to the skills and talents of Irish people, without being capital intensive. It has made several videos of its own.

The Roman Catholic Church was among the first institutions in Ireland to realise the potential of television when in the 1950s Archbishop John Charles McQuaid of Dublin allowed two priests to learn about it in the USA, leading to the *Radharc* programmes which are shown regularly on RTE and the Communications Centre at Booterstown in Dublin which was started to train clergy in media presentation.

Bunny Carr, broadcaster and former head of the Communications Centre, went on to set up Carr Communications. He turned the infant industry into big business showing nearly every politician and business leader in the country how to perform on television. The improved quality of party political broadcasts has been one result.

Television and video are still quite new toys with a novelty value which enhances their ability to communicate. But one should not neglect the older media such as print which, despite the predictions of a paperless society, are far from disappearing.

"TV and print are a partnership", says Judith Brush, communications consultant. "Video is not a stand-alone medium. TV delivers the headlines, print, the detail".[27]

A ten-minute video might cost £2,000 a minute to produce, but that is a minimum. A full corporate video can cost well into six figures. It is better not to do it at all than to try it too cheap.

Four to five weeks is an average production schedule, plus the time that one spends with the client to approve the various stages. Start to finish can be a few months.

One must maintain good communication with the production company at all times, having a clear brief and sticking to it. While more than 90 % of the work is handed over to the production company, things have to be watched, the words fitting the pictures, and the right balance between instruction and entertainment.

"Many problems stem from the person briefing us not knowing his or her own corporate strategy", says Des Good, a producer. "Then there is the problem of conservatism".[28]

VNRs have not really arrived in Ireland yet. They are merely televised coverage supplied to the television station without charge in the same way as a press release.

Where they are common, stations' attitudes vary, sometimes using them enthusiastically and sometimes distrusting them as propaganda. Ultimately they welcome them because with squeezed budgets and reduced staff they cannot get camera crews to all of the events which they would like to cover.

The VNR has obvious uses for damage limitation at time of crisis, but if it is to succeed, it has to be as objective as what the station's own camera crew would shoot. Exxon felt after the Valdez oil spillage in Alaska that their side of the story was not getting across, so they sent out a VNR.

While television programmes, on one's own satellite network, are very effective, they are only suitable for some global corporations. Few organisations have the same use for them as the US-firm Federal Express which sends a daily information update to its 80,000 employees over its own satellite network. But other uses are limitless: Washington politicians issue excerpts from their speeches, or comments on current issues packaged in video form and beamed back home to local television stations; Merrill Lynch advised 50,000 customers through a satellite TV hook-up on how to invest their money and the Ford, General Motors and Chrysler motor companies update distributors on new products.

In the UK, the Whitbread brewery showed areas of their operation which had performed particularly well and sent them out with the annual report as background for the business programmes and interviews with senior executives.

Greenpeace have a camera-crew at all of their protests, often extremely dangerous ones. Within minutes of the action, the footage is beamed around the globe from the satellite relay station based on board the group's flagship.

What benefits do organisations see in expenditure of this sort? One advantage is the ability to direct unfiltered communication to employees. Also, there is greater credibility, with people more likely to believe what they see on television. They do not just read the chief executive's words - they see her eyes, hear her inflection and notice her attitude.

There are benefits in the speed of preparation and transmission, attractive for a global corporation which wants to speak quickly to all of its staff or customers, but there are dangers. Says consultant Marianne Allman: "The video business is a risky form of corporate roulette: you put your money up front and you have to take what you get. The losers include clients who have bought programmes to find that once completed, the videos do not satisfy their original brief. And there are those who have commissioned a programme only to discover that video was not the medium they needed"[29].

24. Sponsorship

A REPORT prepared for the Royal Philharmonic Orchestra in 1974
described sponsorship as "the donation or loan of resources (men,
money, materials, etc) by private individuals or organisations to
other individuals or organisations engaged in the provision of those
public goods and services designed to improve the quality of life"[30].
    Sponsorship has a long history and in Renaissance times, as
to-day, it provided great benefits for the community. Some of the
finest works of art and music would not exist had it not been for
wealthy princes and popes.
    Sponsorship is given with the expectation of a benefit in
return. This distinguishes it from patronage which does not seek a
return either in money, business or praise.
    It is a business decision, an investment. "In essence, modern
sponsorship is a mutually beneficial business arrangement between
sponsor and sponsored to achieve defined objectives", writes Victor
Head[31].
    Nearly £20 million a year is spent on sponsorship in Ireland,
two thirds of it on sport. Multiply by 12 to get a UK figure and by 35
to guess what US companies spend.
    A survey in 1985 showed that 65 % of the top Irish firms were
involved in sponsorship. 39 % of the sponsorships were run directly
by tobacco companies, and 16 % by drinks companies. The most well-
known sponsorship was the Carroll's Irish Open golf championship.
Running now for nearly 30 years, it has been the greatest success of
all Irish sponsorships[32].
    Exposure of the company name and display of its corporate
identity features, especially on television, is the most common reason
for sponsorship.
    Cornhill Insurance, who had never spent more than £25,000
a year on advertising, decided in 1977 to spend £1 million over the
next five years sponsoring the cricket test matches in England. They
were a small, relatively unknown company, with only 2 % of the
population being aware of them before they went into the sponsorship. Before a penny had been spent, merely through the repeated

announcement of this first seven-figure deal for cricket, this recognition had jumped to 8 %. It later settled at 17 % making Cornhill the third most well-known insurance company in the UK. Also, for an expenditure of £1 million over the first five years, increased in subsequent renegotiations and still running, Cornhill has increased its market share, not least through massive support from the cricket community.

Sponsors want their name included in the title of the event and for many years newspapers resisted. Now, however, even the quality papers and the BBC use sponsors' names freely. Sponsors who are also big advertisers have more chance of their name being used. *The Irish Times* uses the sponsor's name for the first mention only in each story.

Some names do not sound well in the title and because they are awkward they soon cease to be used. The Barclay's League, the Budweiser Irish Derby and the Carroll's Open Golf sound all right but when the League of Ireland got their major football competition sponsored by a fast food company it did not sound well as the Pat Grace Famous Fried Chicken League.

Assessment of sponsorship will often hinge around measurement of how often the company name was mentioned, the logo shown etc.

Sponsors should not always expect immediate results. A sponsorship is not like an advertising campaign. The impact will often be over a long period. It will take people some time to associate the sponsor with the event.

Sponsorship is not a substitute for advertising. Mention of the name, sight of the logo, will never substitute for the skilled presentation of the advertising message, but one effect can be to make an advertising campaign more effective.

A second reason for sponsorship is corporate hospitality, the opportunity to bring customers and contacts to an event which will be interesting and mutually enjoyable. Better business may result from a social day in relaxed surroundings, fortified by good food and wine.

What has been good for business is becoming an abuse and ruining major sporting events, with the ubiquitous tents and people who have no appreciation of what is happening. In the UK, events like Wimbledon tennis, Lord's cricket, Ascot racing and Henley rowing have been taken over by the corporate entertainers with scant regard for the ordinary fan. The whole charade was deservedly sent up by journalist Frank Keating in a BBC television documentary.[33]

In addition to name exposure and corporate hospitality, sponsors hope to get some reflected goodwill from the event. It helps their reputation to be associated with a good cause, like helping young musicians to buy their instruments, or providing a facility for a hospital. They don't want an unpopular association. Wang dropped Irish rugby sponsorship because of contact with South Africa and Digital Computers almost did the same.

Tobacco companies sponsor because they are restricted from so many forms of advertising. Their product is harmful to health, therefore they like to be associated with events which promote good health.

The Ford Motor Company closed its Cork factory in 1984 and immediately launched into a massive local and national sponsorship of sport and the arts. On the day the factory closed with nearly 2,000 people thrown out of work, the headlines in *The Cork Examiner* featured the closure but a wraparound supplement hailed the weekend concert, *Siamsa Cois Laoi*, which the company was sponsoring. They then sponsored the national leagues in hurling and gaelic football, bringing their name into every parish in the country. It was a cynical use of sponsorship money, but it worked; criticism over the closure was muted, the Lord Mayor and other public officials got up to thank the company for its generosity, and the managing director acknowledged that all of his objectives had been achieved[34].

In choosing a sponsorship, look for one that is suitable to the organisation. The audience must be right and participation must be seen to enhance both the products and the reputation. Make sure that it fits in with corporate plans, that it can be afforded and that there is sufficient expertise to make the event a success. A motor rally might not be the best sponsorship for a manufacturer of children's toys, but it can be ideal for a motor manufacturer or supplier of motor parts. Nissan sponsor a cycle race, not because they expect cyclists to move over to cars but because a tour of the country, televised every day, passes through so many towns and villages where the company has dealers. Nissan's original target in this sponsorship was to get recognition for the name change from Datsun. They have spent over a million pounds to date and they believe it is working for them.

The total cost of a sponsorship can be up to three times the basic outlay. For every £1,000 donated, another £1,000 will be spent backing up the event with advertising, merchandising and marketing. Up to a further £1,000 will be the effective cost of staff involvement.

Sponsorship does not have to cost millions. Carroll's started a competition for the professional press photographers and, for only a fraction of what they spend on golf, they have got an excellent return in coverage of company activities and in goodwill.

It can be better to sponsor an event than a team or individual. If it is well-run the event will bring glory regardless of who wins, but if one sponsors, say boxer Barry McGuigan, like Irish Permanent Building Society did, it is all right while he is winning but not when he is floored and the referee counts over his head with the world's television cameras focused on the sponsor's banners and logos.

Sponsors very often set up a new award. But beware. There are now too many awards. Padraig Flynn, TD, Minister for Justice, has said that companies would be better spending their money creating jobs than piling up one award after another and gaining "only cheap Brownie points"[35]. The first award of its type is the one which is remembered. For writers, there is the Booker Prize which gets massive publicity every year. But there are many other book awards of which most of the public are ignorant. And, even then, who is Booker ? Very few people seem to know.[36] So, what is the point of the sponsorship ? Does it sell more product ?

It is not enough to throw money at an event and hope for the best. Once the sponsor is in there people will associate her with it, for good or for bad. She must take over the event and make it a quality product, as Budweiser did with the Irish Derby. The event was slipping, with falling attendances, until Budweiser realised its value in prime time television in the US and for the Irish launch of their beer.

Sponsorships can fail and sponsors can feel very sore at

wasting their money. But whether they fail or not, there should in the first instance be a firm contract so that both sides know what is expected. Sponsorships should be for a fixed period with a review before renewal. Once objectives have been achieved there may not be any point in continuing.

Sponsorship is of concern not just to the sponsor who has to make a business decision about the thousands of requests which she gets. It is also a major business activity for those who are sponsored. And many of them do not know how to set about getting it.

To start with, they should select carefully a sponsor who will fit their proposed product or activity. An insurance company is unlikely to sponsor a high risk activity like hang-gliding; nor would a bank be interested in a gambling competition. They should then draw up a document clearly stating what the sponsor will be expected to contribute, how she will be involved and what return she can expect.

The best sponsor to seek might not always be one of the old reliables like Guinness, or Bank of Ireland or Irish Life. Guinness, for instance, have 600 sponsorships going at any one time, from tankards for pub quiz competitions to the large expenditure of the Guinness Jazz Festival in Cork every October bank holiday weekend.

There are, also, other forms of sponsorship apart from money. There can be donation of materials, office facilities, secondment of personnel and so on. These should all be considered in the sponsorship proposal.

Cothú - The Business Council for the Arts, is a body which acts as a broker for businesses wanting to sponsor and individuals or groups needing sponsorship. Cothú has introduced, in association with *The Sunday Business Post,* annual awards to recognise and encourage imaginative and effective business sponsorship of the arts. Each week, over several months, *The Sunday Business Post* publishes a brief article on an arts sponsor.

RTE periodically review their sponsorship guidelines to ensure fair play especially for their advertisers and their audiences. "Sponsorship or indirect funding has become an accepted source of finance for programme making", they say, "It should be a means of enhancing existing programmes or of making programmes which otherwise could not be included in our schedule. Generally, sponsorship should add to our income, but at least should not act to the detriment of advertisement sales"[37].

Sponsorship is not allowed for news or current affairs programmes, nor for religious or agricultural programmes. Smart move, though, by Pitman Moore, the veterinary products company, to sponsor the 6.25 pm radio weather forecast between *Farm Diary* and the News.

25. Exhibitions

AN INCREASE in sales is the main reason for organisations taking part in exhibitions, but there are also public relations benefits if the event is used properly.

Exhibitions are a big international industry. In 1989, in the UK, for instance, £1.3 billion a year was spent on 707 exhibitions which were supported by 100,000 exhibitors and more than 10 million visitors. Of the sales leads generated, 74 % were new[38].

The average cost of a sales lead through an exhibition is £35, compared with anything from £50 to £250 through a sales call. An estimated 80 % of all German trade takes place at exhibitions.

Much of Ireland's export trade results from exhibitions at home and abroad. With support from Bord Trachtála, manufacturers travel the world to display and sell their products.

There must be a good reason for exhibiting. It is sales in most cases, but is this the exhibition which will give the best results ? There are many types of exhibition. Big organisations might hire a hotel or a hall and have a solo show; or it might be a trade show with very defined audience and restricted to one's own industry; or a general show with the public admitted.

It can be a full-dress affair with professionally-built stands, costing a lot of money in materials and furnishings, or it can be lower-key in a hotel room. It can be on its own or in association with a conference with a captive audience.

Consider all of this when designing and preparing the stand. An idea which might grab an audience at the Dublin Spring Show would not necessarily be needed at an exclusive trade showing in Jury's Hotel.

There are some splendid ideas in exhibition design, but they must be an aid to viewing the products and not just a spectacle in a vacuum.

For instance, Spectrum Communications had the right idea when they built the Hewlett Packard stand for Telecom in Geneva, the biggest telecommunications show in the world: "We built the tallest stand in the exhibition. The floor was actually a giant lift which carried the audience up three levels for three different presentations. But the real trick was that the only way down was via the stairs past all the company's exhibits.[39]

Be vigilant as the stand is being built. Contractors have heavy workloads and tight deadlines. They are still hammering the final nails minutes before, or even after, the official opening of the exhibition. Supervise the work and ensure that it is somebody else's nails that come last. Check for every detail that has been agreed to in the original design.

Start preparing in good time. The decision to take part may have been made by marketing, but it is wise for public relations also to be consulted; early involvement improves the chances of publicity.

Be wary of organisers' claims. An estimated 100,000 people may attend, but what chance is there that all of them will visit this stand, or create a sale ? On what basis is the 100,000 figure calculated ? Was a similar exhibition held before ? - talk to some who participated and seek their reaction. What is the track record of the exhibition organiser ? - will she live up to her promises, will she hold the exhibition at all ?

Exhibitors have been concerned that organisers exaggerate the size and classification of audience. The Exhibition Industry Federation in the UK, formed in 1988, now encourages independent audits which can be universally accepted.

Having decided to exhibit, do so with enthusiasm. This applies even when the prestige of waving the flag may be the only reason for being there. If one must go in to wave the flag, make sure that flag waves better than anybody else's.

Make early contact with the exhibition press officer, because her plans may involve features in press and trade publications, material for catalogues and general news angles which will build up interest.

Staff for the stand should be selected carefully. They must be trained to know about the company and its products, talk intelligently to prospective customers and answer queries. The best salesperson, however, is not always the best one for the stand. Often she is the best salesperson because of an ability to move around in the market place and she might feel confined on the stand and lose interest.

Staff must not block the entrance, nor look bored, nor get so engrossed in conversation with each other that the visitor feels like an intruder. Nor should staff be over-attentive. "When I'm at an exhibition the one thing I can't stand is being hassled by staff", says Jack Kessler, a UK consultant.[40]

"Selling at an exhibition requires special skills and techniques, just as telesales or door-knocking do", says journalist Ken Deeks. "Indeed, exhibition selling is often seen as a combination of the two, since it takes place face-to-face, but with a previously unsolicited prospective customer"[41].

Many feel that moving, electronic objects on the stand help catch attention. If there are such attractions, make sure that the staff know how to operate and repair them.

Staff should be alert for unwelcome visitors, competitors posing as possible customers to get sensitive information, and timewasters talking but not buying.

Be alert to the audience and invite all of those whom one wants well in advance. Find out early if some dignitary is opening the exhibition or visiting it. Try to find some reason why she should visit the stand. If the company is a major importer of Californian wine and the US ambassador is visiting, it makes sense for her to visit the stand - if she knows it is there.

Be on the lookout for photo-opportunities. The late Vincent Colgan, public relations manager for An Bord Báinne, the Irish Dairy Board, was wondering how to get attention for Ireland at the Berlin

Green Week, probably the biggest food show in the world. Willy Brandt, then Mayor of Berlin was opening it, but, with hundreds of stands in several massive halls, there was little chance of him seeing the Bord Báinne stand. So, Vincent, armed with a massive ball of Irish cheese, ambushed him at a suitable point on his tour. Before security men could move, but with plenty of time for the cameras to click, he pressed the cheese into Willy Brandt's arms and said: "Mayor Brandt, this is a present from the people of Ireland for the poor people in the city of Berlin".

Feed information and news angles to the exhibition press officer. The occasion can be used to make company announcements, launch new products or make charitable donations. It costs a lot to take part in an exhibition; so make sure that every penny works.

Journalists do not want massive press kits in glossy folders; so do not force them. There is more chance of success with a brief well-written press release. If there are a hundred exhibitors and ninety-nine of them present bulky press kits, the journalist is more likely to read the hundredth one which is a single sheet of newsworthy and interesting information.

Frank Jefkins describes press rooms at exhibitions, chockablock with discarded press kits. He remembers going by train to one exhibition and seeing the press officer wheeling a large trolley down the platform, loaded with press kits[42].

Keep a record of all visitors to the stand. Each one of them can be a potential customer. One simple form of record is a business card competition. Just drop the card into a box to qualify for a prize.

Whatever system is used, the information must be processed quickly and followed up. The exhibition goes on long after the last stand has been dismantled.

Stands and products should be guarded at all times, including the final dismantling. Men in white coats have been known to walk in and load valuable equipment into a lorry, never to be seen again.

If exhibiting regularly, be aware of changing trends. Talk to competitors about their experiences. The Dublin Spring Show, once the prime showcase for farm machinery, has now lost a lot of business to the National Ploughing Championships. Many exhibitors found it too expensive, and swamped by the general public who were never going to be customers.

Notes

1   cf. Tom Bairstow, *Fourth-Rate Estate - An Anatomy of Fleet Street*, Ch. 7 - PR: The Fifth Estate Makes News, Comedia, London, 1985.

2   Pierre Salinger, Lecture to IABC Annual Conference, London, 1987.

3   Bill Maxwell, Lecture at *Appreciation of Public Relations* course, School of Management Studies, College of Commerce, Rathmines, 1992.

4   cf. Nicholas van Zanten, *How to Write a Press Release*, regular two-day course organised by Communications Training plc, London.

5   Basil Saunders and Alexander C. Rae, *Bluff Your Way in PR*, Ravette Books, Horsham, West Sussex, 1991, p. 24.

6   *Nighthawks* the Network 2 television programme on RTE, was set in a pub with drinking, singing and appropriate sound effects. Interviewees sat together at tables, drinking. The interviewer, Shay Healy, moved from one table to another, with just a few words at each. The Sean Doherty piece, alleging that the then Taoiseach, Charles Haughey, was implicated in phone-tapping in 1982, was done from a bar in Roscommon.

7   Robert S. Redmond, *No Need to Shout*, PR Week, 18 February 1988.

8   Andrew Crofts, *Get it in Writing*, PR Week, 27 August 1987.

9   Steve Nickolls, *Do In-House Journals have to be Boring*, PR Week, 13 November 1986.

10   Report on *Industry Week* survey by Gary W.Kemper, *Employee Publications: Are They a Poor Investment for Many Organizations*, Communication World, IABC, San Francisco, April 1991.

11   Tim Aston, *Internal Organs in Poor Way*, PR Week, 21 December 1989.

12   Roy Paul Nelson, *The World of Special Publications*, Communication World, IABC, September 1986.

13   *The Scotsman*, 27 December 1957, quoted in Karin Newman, *Financial Marketing and Communications*, Holt Rinehart and Winston, Eastbourne, UK, 1984, p.8.

14   Eileen Scholes, *Fine Lines*, PR Week, 20 September 1990.

15   John Cole, *Annual Reports*, in Pat Bowman (ed), *Handbook of Financial Public Relations*, Heinemann, Oxford, 1989, p. 22.

16   Lecture to PRII Certificate in Public Relations course, 14 February 1990.

17   Quoted in Jane Greenwald, *Creating Variations on an Annual Theme*, Communication World, IABC, San Francisco, December 1988.

18   Jeremy Myerson, *Making the Words Count*, PR Week, 6 September 1990.

19   John Cole, op. cit, p.33.

20   Alun John, *Picture This*, PR Week, 9 July 1987.

21   *The Guardian*, 19 February 1988.

22   Philip N. Douglis, *PhotoCritique*, Communication World, IABC, September 1986.

23   Philip N. Douglis, *PhotoCritique*, Communication World, IABC, November 1986.

24   Mark Warner, *Getting the Picture*, PR Week, 21 July 1988.

25   Dorothy I. Doty, *Publicity and Public Relations*, Barron's Business Library, New York, 1990, p. 105.

26   cf. Hugh Oram, *Corporate Video: A Guide for the Corporate Client*, The Irish Times, 25 September 1990.

27   cf. Gray Allen, *What's Hot in Corporate TV ?* Communication World, IABC, October 1989.

28   cf. Marianne Allman, *Watch Out There's a Video About*, PR Week, 23 March 1989.

29   Ibid.

30   cf. Victor Head (ed.), *Successful Sponsorship*, Director Books, London, 1988, p. 4.

31   Ibid. p.3.

32   Survey conducted by Wilton Research & Marketing for John McMahon & Partners, 1985.

33   *Racquets at Dawn - Corporate Hospitality*, 1988. Pleads the case for the ordinary fan who, for instance, queues all night to get into Wimbledon, or Lord's and finds the corporate fatcats already there guzzling champagne in the tents and leaving the best seats empty. Memorable is one quote from a tycoon who reacted: "Sod the little man !" Also addresses the black market in tickets with people like

Mike Burton, former rugby union international, prepared to pay up to £1000 to get one for a corporate entertainment client.

34 Documented in RTE television programme, *Slants*, presented by Philip King, 8 December 1985.

35 *Publicity Stunts Criticised*, Irish Times, 21 January 1988. As then Minister for the Environment he was launching a booklet, The Environment, *It's Our Life*, for distribution to schools.

36 "The Booker Prize was set up in 1968 by Booker McConnell, an industrial conglomerate primarily dabbling in sugar, whose literary connections were through copyright ownership of Ian Fleming and Agatha Christie. It has brought them public recognition on a scale rare for a trading company". - Anthony Blond, *The Book Book*, Jonathan Cape, London, 1985, p. 179.

37 *Broadcasting Guidelines for RTE Personnel*, Radio Telefís Eireann, 1989, p. 109.

38 Report by Exhibition Industry Federation quoted in Andrew Dickson, *When to Make an Exhibition of Yourself*, The Independent, 9 September 1990.

39 Paul Swan, managing director, Spectrum Communications, quoted in above article in *The Independent*.

40 Jack Kessler, also quoted in *The Independent*..

41 Ken Deeks, *Going in Search of the Hard Sell*, PR Week, 25 January 1990.

42 Frank Jefkins, *Public Relations Techniques*, Heinemann, London, 1988, ch. 25. Jefkins makes this point also in his other books. To date, he has written more than twenty books on public relations.

Chapter Three

Who Really Matters in Public Relations: The Audiences

26.   Employees

AN ORGANISATION communicates with its employees because it needs them. No matter how excellent the product, or the service, nor how large and enthusiastic the market, one can do nothing without a good team.

Public relations should start with the employees - it is simply a matter of getting one's own house into order first, but too often it does not. Employee communication has been described as the cinderella of public relations[1]. A Market and Opinion Research International (MORI) survey for *The Sunday Times* in 1985 showed that British companies had regressed rather than progressed in their approach to employee communication.

Public relations subdivides its audiences and selects special media and techniques for them. In a large organisation staff may be differentiated by rank or function. There are directors, managers, supervisors, production, sales and administrative staff and so on; or they might be differentiated by location, as in a large national or international organisation.

Every member of staff is equally important. In this example from an American newsletter[2], one manager let employees know how valuable they were:

Xmployxx Communication - Xvxry Pxrson Is Important - "You Arx A Kxy Pxrson"

"Xvxn though my typxwritxr is an old modxl, it works vxry wxll - xxcxpt for onx kxy. You would think that with all thx othxr kxys functioning propxrly, onx kxy not working would hardly bx noticxd; but just onx kxy out of whack sxxms to ruin thx wholx xffort.

"You may say to yoursxlf - Wxll I'm only onx pxrson. No onx will noticx if I don't do my bxst. But it doxs makx a diffxrxncx bxcausx to bx xffxctivx an organization nxxds activx participation by xvxry onx to thx bxst of his or hxr ability.

"So thx nxxt timx you think you arx not important, rxmxmbxr my own typxwritxr. You are a kxy pxrson."

Employee communication is not the exclusive responsibility of the public relations department. Every member of staff is involved and communication takes place in all directions, up, down, across and round about. All are ambassadors, communicating outwards, receiving feedback and influencing reputation.

Communication may be scattered over several departments, but public relations should have a co-ordinating role, so that all speak with one voice. Also, public relations should handle skilled areas for which it has been trained. Staff newsletters, for instance, require journalistic and public relations skills, so they should be left to the professionals in public relations, but this does not always happen. Some organisations insult their staff with the poor quality of newsletters, often written and produced by unskilled people.

Public relations consultants are not usually involved in internal communications, except for newsletters. This is probably best, because internal communications need the insider, whose antennae are alert and tuned in to the grapevine.

There must be systems for continuous, two-way communication with staff. Bigger organisations are more likely to realise this, but the smaller ones need to pay attention also. When there are only two or three people together, they all know what is going on, but when they add a few more staff, this open attitude tends to break down, at first imperceptibly.

Personnel departments, involved in recruitment, induction, contracts, pension schemes, sick leave and holiday arrangements, training and so on, are obvious communicators with staff. But they need back-up from public relations, as do all of the other departments. In a sense, the public relations manager is like a consultant, with each of the departments as clients. She examines their needs and provides solutions, for example, personnel fact-files, induction literature, product launches, sales videos, production training manuals.

Staff value communication, often more than salary, and they want to know more than their legal entitlements - more about the organisation, its performance, its future plans. This is where communication tends to leave the personnel department and become the responsibility of other senior managers and of the chief executive. The best public relations is to have an open system of management, to keep staff fully informed about everything.

Many forms of spoken, written and electronic communication are used. Memos and telephones are so common that staff often take them for granted. The memo can be a terrible timewaster, written not to get a message across quickly, but to enable some person up the line to keep herself covered. Staff noticeboards are useful, but must be properly controlled with somebody responsible for looking after them. Different colours could be used each week.

Some experts say that MWA - management by walking about - is the best form of communication. Feargal Quinn gives his supermarket managers small, uncomfortable offices, so that they will be more encouraged to walk about and meet both staff and customers[3].

When Lee Iacocca went in to save the Chrysler motor company in the US, he abandoned the hierarchical idea of management and invited people at all levels to help him. He toured the shop floor to find out the views and ideas of his workers and to ask them to stand alongside him in the battle. He made it clear that the company's strength was its people. He realised that the man in the production line knew more about his 15 square feet of the Chrysler operation than Iacocca himself could hope to know and he respected that knowledge.[4]

Staff should be encouraged to participate in corporate decisions, their ideas welcomed, discussed and taken on board when good.

Important communication takes place through informal settings, such as parties and outings. Management should encourage these and listen without rancour to the home truths which frequently slip out.

Management must tune in to the grapevine and be aware that the more outrageous the rumour the faster it spreads and the more likely it is to be believed. Make sure that the grapevine is kept well-informed. Hard facts are the best antidote to rumour.

Staff should be the first to hear what is of importance to them. Reading it in the newspaper is not enough.

When the news is bad, no amount of management bluff can pretend otherwise. If 300 jobs are to go, this cannot be hidden from the unfortunate 300. It is little consolation to them that their departure will save the company and return it to profit. But, there are ways to prepare for and break the news and to follow it up with professional advice and counselling.

Management must be prepared to communicate directly with staff, going above, but not excluding, the unions. There remains a vital role for unions, but never to be the exclusive means of communication between management and staff.

Absence of unrest does not necessarily mean that staff communications are good. Silence may be apathy, dry fuel waiting for the spark of industrial trouble to set it alight.

During industrial disputes, public relations will be closely involved in communicating with the media and other outside audiences, but the manager should not go into open combat for management against staff. She is manager of public relations for the whole organisation, and not just a management spokespiece.

Larger organisations find merit in the communication audit. A specialist, usually an outside consultant, examines all of the communications structures and patterns and reports with recommendations, applying the same rigour and objectivity as a chartered accountant on the financial audit. She looks at all relationships and how they are effected by communications. She works by observation, questionnaire, interview and group meetings, and walking about.

The auditor must treat all staff equally. She is brought in by the chief executive, but the answers that she seeks are as likely to be with the porter at the back door as with the chief executive. She needs the full co-operation of both management and staff.

If one values the communication audit, be prepared to spend money on it. It can take months, with questionnaires, interviews, interim reports, further meetings. People must be encouraged to talk, to discuss in groups - not with any fear of being under the microscope or their jobs being threatened. The well-conducted audit, enthusiastically acted upon, should make the workforce happier, more productive and more fulfilled and the company more profitable[5].

27. Community

COMMUNITY relations are a feature of most public relations programmes, but more likely than any other not to be followed through. This is regrettable, because public relations is about being socially responsible, the conscience of the company, and ensuring that it acts always in the public interest.

No business can be an ivory tower or a barricaded fortress, shut off from its neighbours. They might not know anything about its highly technical operations but they are the people nearest to it and include many of its present and future employees. They breathe the same air, clean or foul, drink the same water, pure or polluted.

The world is getting smaller, so that all are now neighbours. Chernobyl is in The Ukraine, but when its nuclear plant exploded the whole world knew about it, and cared, as radiation spread, affecting even Welsh sheep.

Community relations are a permanent presence, even if an organisation chooses to ignore them. To care for them is like an insurance policy. It might cost money now, but one never knows when a claim will have to be made. An organisation might think that a quiet community is one at peace with it, but when there is a tricky planning permission, it might, at great cost, regret that it never did anything about that smell, or the rat-infested site.

Do not ever take community relations for granted, but work at them and see them as an opportunity to make the organisation better respected and more successful. People like to work for and do business with a company which is seen to care.

Attention to community relations has been forced upon international companies, especially in the Irish pharmaceutical industry which is now one of the top 12 exporters in the world.

US giant, Merck Sharp & Dohme battled for ten years from 1978 to prove that emissions from their factory, in south Tipperary, were not to blame for the poor health of farmer John Hanrahan and of his animals. They won their case in the High Court but the ruling was overturned by the Supreme Court. Eventually, they paid compensation that was between their offer of £500,000 and John Hanrahan's claims of £1.8 million for nuisance caused by factory emissions and ill-health to Hanrahan and his farm animals. The estimated total cost to the company was £5 million. MSD still insist on their innocence and are confident that their plant is absolutely safe. They are near completion of a £13 million programme to reduce waste emission. In 1992, they won the EOLAS Good Environment Management Award for their "explicit measurable objectives for good environmental practice".

This was a complex case and MSD were criticised for a low-key public relations approach and for allowing John Hanrahan to beat them in the publicity battle. At the start they probably feared a snowball effect if they had conceded the case and made a settlement out of court, but one strange feature was that neighbouring farms do not seem to have suffered. MSD argued that the misfortunes of the Hanrahan farm were caused by poor farm management.

Another US pharmaceutical, Merrill Dow, after long argument, won their legal battles and got their planning permission but did not build their factory at Killeagh, 25 miles east of Cork because of local opposition. That was the real reason although they claimed that a merger in the US made the new factory unnecessary. They lost a lot of money. Their timing, though, was unfortunate, the application for planning permission being lodged ten days after the Supreme Court judged in the Hanrahan case. Their public relations weakness was in failing to convince the local community in advance of planning permission.

Shortly after, the Swiss multinational, Sandoz, already with the corporate blemish of a serious accident in Basle, in 1986, avoided the mistake of Merrill Dow. They ensured local support before they started their £150 million investment at Ringaskiddy, near Cork harbour, on a 90-acre site owned by the IDA. In a long public relations campaign, organised jointly by Robin O'Sullivan in Cork and Pat Keating of Grayling, in Dublin, they fully informed local people and interested groups, even bringing them to their plant in Switzerland, so they could not be accused afterwards of trying to pull wool across anybody's eyes. They asked EOLAS, the National Science and Technology Agency, to conduct an environmental impact study. They got their planning permission, and their factory, and the support of the people, a *Cork Examiner*/Irish Marketing Surveys opinion poll showing 57 % of people in Cork in favour of the development with 20 % against and 23 % holding no opinion. A referendum in the Ringaskiddy area also indicated a clear majority in favour.

Sandoz learnt from the mistakes of others but so did the planning authorities. Cork County Council, in December 1989, placed an unprecedented 70 conditions on the Sandoz planning permission and An Bord Pleanála imposed another 28 before building began.

The reward for good community relations, as in the case of these chemical companies, can be great, but the price of failure can be even greater.

David Holden estimates that a good community campaign can very quickly soak up £100,000, because it is labour intensive and there are not any short cuts. He says the major concern for public relations in the early days, when opposition inevitably forms, is to prevent complaints mounting to such a pitch that there has to be a public inquiry which will be expensive and time-consuming, even if successful at the end.[6]

The campaign has to be planned meticulously, like a war. And it must concentrate first on those living nearest to the development.

Sandoz proved the importance of this when they got the support of the most immediate local residents at a time when opponents ten miles away were protesting strongly.

First, inform fully all who might have an interest in the development. Tell them what is involved. Respond to their anxieties, respect them and do not dismiss them as cranks.

The support of local groups is essential, but identify those who really matter. Give them as much information as possible. Show that there is nothing to hide. Take them into one's confidence.

This assumes, of course, that the client, or the board of directors, are being straight with their public relations manager. They must be prepared to face and answer all of the awkward questions and to tell the truth.

There will always be objectors to a major project and the Irish planning system is designed to ensure that they are allowed their voice. These objectors are usually well-informed and have done their research, so that it is never enough to give them half-truths. Don't underestimate their grasp of the important issues.

Do not waste time trying to change the hard core group of objectors, but go to those whom they are influencing. Also, those who shout loudest are not always the most important.

The information campaign must be backed up by literature , presentations and meetings, but these must never be over-elaborate, nor should there be excessive hospitality or suggestions of trying to buy off the opposition.

Pay attention to one-to-one communication with small groups, rather than mass meetings where demagogues can too easily take over. Have spies on the ground who will report what the people are really thinking and saying.

Community relations for a new company, especially in the chemical and mining industries, do not stop when the opposition has been beaten and planning permission given. There follows the construction phase, with apologies for the nuisance being caused, and the need to keep all parties, especially the former objectors, fully informed.

Make peace with these objectors. Their support will be needed as recruitment takes place and the new factory matures alongside its neighbours. She who was spy during the planning stage can now be troubleshooter, anticipating problems and continuing to keep in touch with the grassroots.

People expect good neighbourliness from those whose operations affect them. They expect the local council, the ESB, Bord Gais and Telecom to apologise for inconvenience caused by roadworks, but these companies can turn it to their advantage by showing the positive benefits which the whole community will get from the improvements under way. Indeed, people were more relieved than annoyed by the hundreds of roadworks in Dublin after the Raglan House gas explosion in 1987. It meant that something was being done, even belatedly, to remove the time bombs that were those old pipes under the streets.

Good relations means being honest when a problem occurs. If one runs a nuclear plant and there is a leak, however tiny, announce it before it is dragged out and exaggerated by gossip. Have an open door policy for visits from local people and journalists. If it is a sizeable operation have open days to explain and illustrate what you are doing.

British Nuclear Fuels responded to criticisms of their operation at Sellafield by building a large visitors' centre and making the plant a major tourist attraction. It did not eliminate people's concern, nor make future spillages impossible, but it showed the company was responding to public concern and trying to do something.

Good relations means involvement in the community. This can include organising social events, children's parties, old folks christmas dinners, sponsorships, offering facilities to local groups. Some companies have a contingency fund and a committee through which they make these small local sponsorships.

Respond to students who request information for projects. See them not as a nuisance but an opportunity. Be prepared for them and have stocks of up-to-date literature. Take pride that they are coming to the company.

Encourage managers to become local leaders. Some organisations require their top executives to live near their work. This shows that they are genuine neighbours. The managing director who joins the delegation to the minister to complain about a new motorway plan will do more for the company than any number of prizes at local fetes. Corporate advertising can get the community message across. The international computer company, Amdahl, moved to Swords, Co. Dublin in 1980 and ten years later they marked their anniversary with an advertisement: "A Commitment to our Community", with "our" underlined. It took pride that "ten years on we have continued to grow with our local community. As one of Swords' leading employers, Amdahl Ireland, is actively involved with the community through the support of educational, environmental and social activities. At Amdahl we value our relationship within our community. Future growth and development will continue to enhance this relationship as Amdahl consistently meets the superior quality standards of our customers.[7]

All of the measures taken to show that one is a good neighbour are useless if they are only cosmetics; useless if staff are treated badly and not given decent pay and conditions, useless if the product is bad, or the local river is polluted.

28. Customers

IN BUSINESS, the customer should come first. That is obvious. Or is it ? What about a communist state where there is no competition ?

Every ten years or so, management writers re-discover the customer as if they had just invented the wheel. Praise is then heaped upon some manager who has made it her motto. Feargal Quinn, managing director of Superquinn, is the latest. His book, *Crowning the Customer*, explains how he practices his excellent, but simple philosophy.

Some organisations do not put their customers first. They even put them last, as with banks refusing for years to open at lunch-time or in the evening, as a result of union resistance.

Trade unions can be an obstacle in customer relations. Their customer is their member, not the person who buys the product or the service. They will strike when it hurts the customer most and they

I

will use her as a wedge to get concessions from the company. Unions fail to realise that their members' jobs only exist because there are customers.

Schools and universities may fail to identify their customer - the student. Courses are products and as with any other product the customer, the student, must be happy. But the administration of grants, the provision of facilities, the imposition of regulations, often give the impression that the student is a nuisance in the way of bureaucrats happily twisting themselves in red tape.

Public relations is not the only management function involved with the customer. Marketing is its close partner in this area. Marketing identifies the customer, discovers what she wants and gives it to her, and advertising persuades her to buy. Public relations tells her more about the product, arousing her interest and creating the environment in which the entire activity can succeed.

Lyons introduced round teabags and ran an advertising campaign that was, to most people, silly. If they had backed up the campaign with public relations, they could have told an interesting story as to how research showed round bags to be better than square ones.

There is often confusion as to the separate roles of public relations and marketing in dealing with the customer. Some examples can help.[8]

The American Pet Food Institute wanted to expand the market for pet food. For marketing, the objective was to increase pet food sales and the strategy was to increase dog and cat ownership. For public relations, the objective was to persuade people to acquire a pet and the strategy was to communicate the benefits of pet ownership. So, public relations concentrated on the joys and rewards of owning a pet. It included contests, exhibitions, research, expert spokespersons, publications and national and local publicity.

Campbells wanted people to drink more soup. That was the marketing objective, but public relations had to give people new reasons for drinking soup. So, the public relations strategy was to publicise research about soup being good food and aligning it with healthy lifestyles. It included national publicity, spokespersons, videos, publications, competitions.

In customer relations, the brand itself is often the corporate entity. The asset value of brands is now realised and taken into account when, for instance, takeover bids are mounted and share prices set. Independent Newspapers have revalued their titles at £104 million, an increase of £56 million on the previous valuation. This was not an arbitrary or a cosmetic exercise, but done professionally by Hambros, the London financial company. On the other hand, Dublin businessman, Mike Hogan, was able to buy the title of *In Dublin*, the collapsed listings magazine, for £6,000.

Large organisations use separate teams for marketing and for public relations for each brand, as if they were separate companies within the group. One company can have competing brands. Guinness, for example, brew or distribute numerous competing beers and lagers and Proctor & Gamble and Lever Bros are forever launching new washing powders in competition with themselves and with each other.

Brands are sensitive, because customers can be very fickle. Massive sums are spent on market research to get the exact answers to such questions as how the brand is performing, the emotional attitudes which it creates, whether it is seen as a market leader or an also ran and the kind of people with whom it is associated.

If there are negative attitudes to say, Japanese cars, drinks in cans, cigarettes and so on, it is one function of public relations to counter them, or to advise that they are insurmountable. At the height of apartheid in South Africa, it would have been futile to persuade people who had boycotted oranges from that country to go back to them. Nothing could change until apartheid was abolished and reforms set in motion to make South Africa a democratic country.

Media coverage can be an effective strategy in reaching the customer, but difficult, because editors do not want to publish plugs for products. They want news angles. One London company runs seminars on "How to get press coverage for unnewsworthy products".[9]

When a new product is being launched the media want balanced information, not sales literature. They want details of market research, genuine angles on how the new product is different, trade news on its packaging, distribution and promotional details.

Feature articles are prepared, and interviews set up, so that when the launch comes, and the advertising starts, the market is ready. A party of journalists may be brought to visit the factory and see the new process and learn how it has been developed. Typical of this is the facilities offered to motoring journalists to test drive new models.

Often the marketing programme itself can be news. There might be teaser advertisements leading up to the launch, as when Town of Monaghan Cooperative Society was launching its range of Mona yogurts. For weeks in advance it ran a poster campaign about Ed loving Mona. People asked questions and just when curiosity had been suitably aroused, the product was launched.

It can be bad public relations to run a campaign that merely shocks. Benetton get publicity for distasteful posters which bear no relation to their clothes, but it must be questioned whether they get goodwill, or improve the environment in which they can sell the clothes. They certainly do not make new friends.

Celebrities can be used to enhance a launch. Avonmore Foods introduced a new dairy spread but there was nothing unusual about it, as several competitors had already done the same. But when TV presenter Noel Edmonds attended the launch at an 11 am breakfast in a Dublin hotel, there was a full attendance of journalists and all wrote with enthusiasm about the event and the product.

The role of public relations in assisting the sales force should not be neglected for this is the immediate link with the customer, the voice of the customer for those sitting at desks.

The customer should be listened to because she uses the product. Market research cannot substitute for the individual customer. If her experience seems to contradict the professional findings, listen to her, she may be right. She may be the tip of an iceberg, of other customers who think the same.

Superquinn use customer panels, inviting volunteer groups to meet Feargal Quinn. They raise all aspects of the company operation and offer ideas for improvement. Quinn acknowledges that ideas for action come from these panels and that problems are anticipated and often prevented.

To some the public relations person is the smooth talker whose job is to listen to complaints, defend the organisation and do nothing.

Complaints must be listened to and acted upon, no matter how embarrassing.

Marie Jennings, consultant in consumer affairs, wants every company to set up a customer complaints department and to name it as such. "It's incredible, but many companies claim they do not get complaints", she says. "Of those companies which have set up a complaints service for their customers, more often than not it's just a fudge - lip service."

She adds that "research in the US has proved that it is four times more expensive to gain a new customer than it is to win round a disaffected one. Deal with a complainer well and she'll stay loyal and even recommend you to others".[10]

Public relations often has to respond to complaints before the full facts are to hand. The best tactic may sometimes have to be to stall, but it is an event that should be prepared for. There can be standard responses, expressing regret when deaths have taken place and assuring that there will be a full enquiry, or regretting the disruption being caused by a strike. Any impression of reluctance or backtracking or lying will be noticed immediately.

Some say the customer is always right, even when she is wrong. When wrong, however, don't tell her or you will humiliate her and lose her as a future customer. Feargal Quinn speaks about the boomerang effect - a happy customer is a repeat customer and one must always work for that, even in the funeral business.

Never seem to make grudging concessions to the rights of customers. Be ahead of government legislation. If it is a supermarket, don't wait until forced to respond to customer concern over the environment and the removal of CFCs, for instance. Welcome the move to greener products. See it not as a restriction on business but as an opportunity to beat the competition.

Good companies do not run purely for profit, although profit is essential if they are to stay in business. In an ethical society, economic activity will be directed towards the wellbeing of the people as well as towards profit. Business must contribute to the betterment of the people and that includes customers.

The company must not knowingly harm its customers and if a product is found to be faulty there must never be cover-up. As soon as there is the slightest risk, the customer must come first, and the product must be withdrawn, no matter what the short-term loss of profit. However, if it is withdrawn it must be with the intention of returning it in an improved form.

Such action has to be prompt. Otherwise it will seem that the company is weighing up the case and balancing customer welfare against profits.

29. Business

BUSINESS audiences are, to mix metaphors, the heart which pumps the blood to an organisation on one hand, and the avenue to the market on the other. As ambassadors they can carry a valuable endorsement of credibility.

They include suppliers, distributors, retailers and even competitors and they cannot be ignored or taken for granted. They can be interchangeable - one organisation's distributor may be another's supplier, a competitor today may be a partner tomorrow.

Suppliers include sources of raw materials, components, print and packaging, fuel, transportation and finished goods. They can also be providers of professional services.

Distributors and retailers are a very broad group and, to quote Jefkins, they may include "brokers, factors, wholesalers, cash and carry warehouses, rack-jobbers, supermarkets and chain stores, co-ops, neighbourhood shops, own shops, appointed dealers, clubs, hotels and holiday centres, mail order or direct response traders, direct salesmen, tally men (credit traders), exporters and overseas importers.[11]

The salesforce is a key link with these business audiences. Public relations is not responsible for sales, but must understand and respect their importance and use its own skills and resources to assist them.

For instance, public relations has an input into sales promotions and sales conferences, and similar platforms where the organisation is on display. Sales representatives appreciate an organisation that communicates well and listens to them. They need good corporate and product literature. Public relations can assist the presentation of the sales message.

Public relations staff who write newsletters can benefit from the experience of the sales staff; and should even accompany them at times on sales calls to see what it is really like. Sales staff are sources of news about the organisation, because they get reactions at first hand, not distilled through management reporting systems.

Some have only one strategy towards suppliers; drive as hard a bargain as possible, and the smaller they are the tougher they are treated. Supermarkets, in particular, are accused of this, especially with small suppliers for whom they are the major, if not the monopoly customer. Drive them as low as possible and if they squeal, cut them off. Drag them so low on price that they cannot make a profit, delay payment beyond normal credit terms knowing there is little they can do about it. The Director of Consumer Affairs recently took one company to court alleging such behaviour.

This is a short-sighted approach. Big supermarkets need their suppliers. They should see them as ambassadors. Reputation, as well as sales, depends upon their endorsement. It might not seem that they are needed now, but what will happen if there are problems? Will they feel any debt of loyalty to the big bully who has tossed them about ? Unlikely.

All suppliers are important. No matter how good the machine, nor efficient the work force, nor keen the price, one small supplier can ruin the whole enterprise. If she is late with delivery, or gives preference to another customer, is it because she has been tossed about in the past and taken for granted ?

Distributors are the face of the manufacturer and the avenue to the retailer. They should be fully briefed about the company, its products and its plans. Give them advance warning of product, packaging changes, special offers and the like. Do not have them hearing it first from the grapevine or the press.

They are also ambassadors. If they have scruffy vans, unmannerly drivers, arrive late, run out of stock, it rubs off on the manufacturer and business is lost.

The motor industry has been particularly competitive in getting and retaining dealerships. Many a tough war has been contested by the big three in the US, General Motors, Ford and Chrysler.

The distributor, or dealer, is probably the most important motoring audience. To the driver, the Zonka dealer is Zonka. It is she who convinces the customer that Zonka is best for her. It is she who looks after the follow-up services, takes the complaints, influences how that motorist will talk to her friends and how she will purchase next time.

Manufacturers can offer incentives to their distributors - competitions, holidays abroad, marketing supports, joint sponsorships. The loyalty of the distributor is vital. Taking the motor industry, again, the distributor may be big and respected. She may be the big Zonka person in her town, but that will exclude her from the rival Robka. If Zonka don't play fair with her, if they take her for granted, they may soon find that she has left them and got a better deal from Robka. That big garage at the centre of the town is now selling Robkas and where is Zonka ? Ask anybody in the street and they don't even know. Distributors are a key target for public relations.

Take the pub-owner. How can she stock and give equal presentation to all of the drink brands which are pressed upon her? For draught beer, she can only fit so many taps on her counter. If a new one comes on the market and her customers want it, she has to let her worst brand drop off at the other end. If she runs out of one, what does she recommend as an alternative to the hesitating customer ?

To many the retailer is the customer. If she does not stock the product and display it properly it will not sell. Have a feedback system with her. Learn from her, because she can tell more home truths about a business than any number of advisers and consultants. She needs to know because she has to take customers' queries directly. She does not want to be caught off-guard and made to look a fool. She is let down badly if a new product is featured in advertisements before she has been told about it. It is a case where effective public relations in advance of advertising and marketing is essential to create the right environment for selling.

The 200 Irish publishers bring out about 1,200 books a year, sizeable, but nothing compared to the UK with its 60,000 new titles each year. To get these books, effectively thousands of competing brands, to the reader, publishers need sales people, distributors, book editors and booksellers and these must all be told in good time what is coming. Publishers must be prepared to pay for promotional aids so that the distributor and the retailer, as well as the reader is enthused.

The best communications with business audiences is often verbal. Have proper systems for meeting them, getting feedback and acting on it.

Sales and general information brochures are a form of business communication, but they must speak to their audience. The retailer does not want the glossy consumer attractions of a new ice-cream. She does not want the advertising hype. But she wants to know in good time how the product is being developed, the terms of sale, the pricing, the margins for her, the packaging, any support for special offers and promotions and so on.

This brings in the trade press. It is read by the trade and it wants to know those finer details which might be boring to the end consumer. The trade reads the advertisements because they can give leads for new business, for better business. Therefore stories which might be construed as puffs in the consumer press could be vital business information in the trade press.

Make it interesting. Organise news stories and features which give advance information, develop angles, highlight the advantages and the applications of new products, new designs. Ask retailers for feedback stories on the use which has been made of the product, get their first-hand accounts of consumer reaction.

Business audiences should be supported in their promotional ventures, in their participation at trade exhibitions, in their sponsorships.

Competitors are an audience; some organisations use public relations first to impress the competition and only secondly to achieve proclaimed objectives. They do not want the competition to think they are slipping or losing their edge. This can lead to futile leapfrogging and special promotions. It is often better to join with competitors to make sense out of these situations. Should we all take part in this exhibition, or are we being exploited by an organiser who wants us to feel individually that if we are not in, people will ask questions about why we are out ? Should we scrap all of these expensive special offers and the hassle that goes with them ?

30.   Politicians

ONE MIGHT ask if there is need for political public relations in Ireland, or for lobbying as it has grown up in the US, Brussels, the UK and elsewhere. Ireland has always been a very politically-conscious country, with easy and informal access to politicians. The multi-seat system keeps them in constant mind of their constituency roots, and if one wants to get through to them, surely the easy informality of the lounge bar or the church gate is sufficient.

It is not enough. There is more to it than might seem on the surface. Irish organisations need to understand the political decision-makers and how to influence them if their interests are to be protected. It is not just the elected politicians who make the decisions, but also the ministerial advisers, the civil servants, the officers of state bodies, the officials of the county council. And do not forget the President. She is above party politics, but her support can be a mighty endorsement with real influence on the decision-makers.

New legislation may be in preparation which could damage an organisation, or it may already have been passed without the consequences being realised. What can be done about it ?

The political scene can be a quagmire and anybody hoping to influence it needs specialist help. Political public relations includes a lot of lobbying, trying to influence the legislators and the decision-makers to act in one's interest and if one can show them that this interest is shared by many other voters, then the battle should be won, because politicians know votes are their lifeblood.

Lobbying can be an ethical minefield. When important issues

and big money are at stake, the temptation to use foul means can be enticing. In the US, where lobbying was born, acquired a murky pedigree and now thrives, there is a strict system of regulation. Everybody knows exactly who is lobbying for whom and how they are paid. Every type of business, every pressure group has its lobbyists and politicians and public servants are bombarded on all sides with the most convincing arguments.

It makes the politician's life harder in one way, but in another she welcomes it because she has no excuse for not being fully informed before she makes a decision.

For the lobbyist, the public relations skills in explaining a case are not enough. Powers of persuasion are needed. And that requires a thorough knowledge of the political system and of how decisions are made, of the legislators and decision-makers and how to influence them.

It is not unethical to seek to influence a politician; indeed it is a healthy part of an open democracy. All interests are entitled to present their case. They always tried but now they are more professional about it and increasingly successful.

Lobbying in the UK is increasing, but in a disorganised way, giving rise to concern. Many lobbyists, not being members of the recognised public relations bodies, are not subject to professional controls. Parliament itself is now planning to regulate them.

Some politicians there believe there is too much lobbying. Labour MP, Bob Cryor, would put all lobbyists up against a wall and shoot them (if it were not for his opposition to capital punishment !), He disagrees with consultants like Nigel Ellis who says "there is not enough lobbying of MPs. Few people understand this and let it go by default, then they wake up to discover that a new piece of legislation restricts their way of living or doing business and complain bitterly".[12]

Ellis says business people ignore the fact of lobbying at their peril. He also points to incredible naiveté and the problem of doing too little too late. For example, Rowntree sent a box of chocolates to every MP when the firm was about to be taken over by a Swiss company. Ellis calls that a "daft gesture".

Lobbying is less intensive in Ireland, but pressure groups are increasingly well-organised and informed. They have been strong on issues like abortion, divorce, the environment, planning permissions for new industries, PAYE taxation and rod licences for fishing. The farming lobby has learnt a lot in the 26 years since it marched on Dublin from all over the country, but was left camping outside the office of the Minister for Agriculture (then Charles Haughey) with nothing for the effort but cold nights under the stars.

Organisations like the Confederation of Irish Industry, the Federation of Irish Employers and the Irish Congress of Trade Unions know all about lobbying and have developed their skills at it.

In consultancy, the foremost lobbyist is Myles Tierney, a former Dublin county councillor. Through his lecturing and writing he has done more than others to promote the idea of lobbying and to show what it can achieve.

One lesson is that those who make the most noise do not always have the greatest success. Banner-waving and marching cannot be the core of the campaign, but only an appendage after all of the other hard work has been done. The students might be marching outside the Minister's office, but the representative of big business may be inside having tea and biscuits with the Minister. No need to ask whose lobbying is being the most effective.

In lobbying, as in any other public relations, the objective must be clear. What is wanted ? - the proposed legislation withdrawn, or amended ? the existing legislation repealed ? the ministerial order witheld, or enforced ? the decision of the county council reversed ? the planning approval granted ?

When the objective is clear one must identify the decision-maker. It will not always be the Taoiseach, nor the Minister. It could be a senior civil servant, or corporation official.

Myles Tierney, in his own formula for organising a lobby, breaks it into three parts.[13]

First, determine that there is an inequality. This will involve research and the preparation of an information booklet, showing that a wrong has been committed or is about to be committed which affects not just one's own interests but those of the wider community. If the county council can be shown that a regulation banning gaming machines in county Dublin will be unjust not only to the people who use these machines as a harmless recreation, but will infringe on everybody's rights, they will give way. But if the other argument is more convincing that some people become addicted to the machines with damage to family and to health, then that side will win. For most political lobbies, there is at the same time a counter lobby.

The good lobbyist can demonstrate that the common good is affected. Myles Tierney speaks about "the public repose". If the lobbyist succeeds in disturbing the public repose, the politician will act to restore it.

Tierney's second step is to dramatise the issue. That is when marches and banner-waving can be effective. There is plenty of scope for publicity stunts here. If one has a good case, dramatise it for all it is worth. French lorry-drivers blocking the motorways in peak tourist season are a nuisance, but can be effective. Too often, students, in particular, dramatise an issue first before anybody else knows what they are on about. Politicians ignore them, knowing that there is not any public support.

Not all issues have to be dramatised. The case is often won at the first stage. Much successful lobbying takes place quietly with cases presented and action following before anybody knows what is happening. In the lead-up to the budget, politicians and civil servants meet the respective pressure groups. That is lobbying. It is part of the consultative process.

Finally, having demonstrated that there is an inequality and having dramatised the issue, Tierney says it is decision-time. Too often lobbyists think they have won the battle when they have convinced the politician and got the promise of action. Promise of action is not itself action. She may have said yes just to get rid of them. They must force her to an irreversible decision. Don't let off the pressure. Push the case to the top of her agenda.

The good lobbyist comes prepared. As in all other forms of public relations, it is a planned process, like a campaign for war. It is mainly persistent hard work. It is also time-consuming and expensive. One is unlikely to get out of even a small professional lobby for less than £50,000, which has led some to question who can do lobbying for the poor, the unemployed and the disadvantaged.[14]

Be ready for all of the answers that the decision-maker may give. Tierney refers to the five denials. The target of the lobby will deny everything, trying each line in turn. She will deny that she has the money, that she has the power, that it is her area of responsibility, that there is sufficient support for the measure or that it would be in the common interest. Finally, if she is beaten on all of these, she will do what politicians do best, she will stall. The best form of stall is to set up a commission to look into the matter. This puts it on the slow burner and ensures that it will be forgotten about and no longer an issue when the commission reports. In the meantime action will be avoided in deference to the work of the commission and not wanting to prejudice its conclusions.

Some lobbyists see power moving from the politicians to the civil servants, the ministerial advisers, the local officials. That may be so, and if one believes the British TV series, *Yes, Prime Minister*, it certainly is so, but the politician is easily miffed. For so long she has seen herself as Ms. Fix-it. Damage her ego unnecessarily and one may suffer the backlash. She might not always be the real decision-maker, but she can be a blocker.

Some think lobbying is merely a matter of writing to the TD. Certainly the number of letters on an issue can influence her and if other TDs get similar approaches, it might convince them that a response is needed. But politicians are not fools, and they quickly realise if they are being used. They get a massive mailbag and claim that 80 % of it, especially computerised letters from lobbying groups, has no effect. But politicians like to know what is going on. The typical Government minister spends 50 % of her time on constituency work, while it is 90 % for the ordinary TD[15].

Irish politicians may, in theory at least, be legislators, but the messenger-boy tradition is so strong with multi-seat constituencies where members of one party are competing against each other, that the politician who ignores the grassroots, might soon not have any grassroots to tend at all.

Pressure groups should certainly involve the elected politicians in their causes. Keep them informed, look for their support, but do not always assume they make the decisions. Find who does and direct the main thrust there.

It can help to know which politicians have a specialist interest in one's own area of business. Get them involved. They can join the lobby; they see themselves as essentially lobbyists.

The focus of lobbying is no longer confined to home. There has been a switch to Brussels, because that is where many decisions are now taken. The farm groups, as well as lobbying at the Minister and her department, now lobby together with them in Brussels to get favourable decisions in the Irish interest.

Some of the best lobbying never has to happen at all. She who is wise has a specialist looking after her interests and giving her early warning of what is coming up. It is another form of crisis planning - act first to prevent it happening. Long before the issue boils over, before the new legislation comes before the house, it can be quietly killed if the consequences are pointed out to the right people. But it all shows the importance of knowing who matters. The busy business executive cannot always do this; she needs her specialist adviser.

To sum up, political lobbying is more than communicating, however skilled and informed one might be. It is also about persuading. The target is not a sitting duck. There are other interests also trying to influence her on a combination of other issues. The lobbyist's approach must be more planned than moving up beside her while she is having a quiet drink, a tactic which is often attempted because of the easy accessibility of Irish politicians.

31.   Financial

FINANCIAL public relations grew more rapidly than any other in the 1980s. In a 1985 survey of British consultants, 34.6 per cent judged it to be their most important area of activity. The next highest response was for marketing support, 21.2 per cent[16].

Much of this public relations seems to be fire brigade activity. The Public Relations Consultants Association in the UK found in 1987 that ad hoc financial work was growing at a rate of more than 120 % per annum, and in some consultancies it accounted for more than 50 % of business[17].

Murray Consultants, from the mid 1970s, were the first Irish company to specialise in financial public relations. Two of their senior directors had been journalists - Joe Murray, financial editor of *The Irish Press* and *The Sunday Independent* and Jim Milton, editor of *Business & Finance*, the leading weekly publication.

The opportunities for financial public relations developed in the UK as large privatisations brought more attention to the money markets and involved the ordinary person in share-buying. There was a spinover into Ireland with privatisations such as Irish Sugar, Irish Life and others to come, as well as highly-profiled company collapses, takeover bids and introductions of new companies to the stock market.

In all cases the public relations advisers have been at the core, with the merchant bankers, stock brokers, accountants and lawyers. Public relations is an essential part of the management team in any corporate finance activity.

The financial audiences cannot be treated as a single group. Different strategies are required for communicating with each of them. They include the private and institutional shareholders, brokers, financial institutions such as banks and insurance companies, fund managers, investment analysts and other investment advisers and financial journalists. A lot of this public relations is face-to-face. One key analyst can make or break the share price, or influence the success of a share issue. Likewise one business editor can influence many readers who are investors.

The public relations adviser needs specialist knowledge and an understanding of financial journalism as well as basic skills. Stock Exchange regulations mean that greater discretion is required than in other areas of public relations and speculation has to be avoided.

Financial journalism is all about money, about the financial performances of companies and the people who run them. Whatever reflects the interests of investors and of taxpayers makes news. There is a great interest in publicly-quoted companies and in banks, insurance companies and stockbrokers, but also in semi-state bodies and issues relating to industry, management, enterprise and entrepreneurial development.

Financial journalists and their readers are not deceived by

glossy presentations and the hype that might go with the launch of a new detergent. They see image-projection for the spoof that it really is. What is of interest to them is company profits, share price and earnings per share. People buy shares in Guinness not because they like black beer but because they believe the company will perform well and give them good returns for their investment.

Financial public relations activity is most visible at time of crisis, but it goes on all of the time. None of these audiences can ever be taken for granted. In the past small shareholders were often neglected and the price was paid when the votes were counted at time of takeover.

The most visible occasions for public relations are the annual general meeting, the annual report, the period leading up to going public, a share issue, a takeover or merger. All of these provide excellent platforms for explaining company performance, demonstrating financial credibility and building confidence amongst the audiences.

Public relations can also enable a company to keep in touch with gossip, whether informed or idle. Rumour can easily rock a volatile market and, if false, must be crushed at source before it gains credence.

Information that could be price-sensitive must, in the interests of all shareholders, be issued to the Stock Exchange first. Announcements of results, for instance, are now made simultaneously to the Stock Exchange and the media. This can be in advance of the annual report which will give the full figures. The Stock Exchange immediately puts it through the computer network so that all interested parties, including the principal journalists, can have it on their desks together.

Insider trading, with some making large gains out of information that is not public knowledge, has always happened. It is only because of the big money now involved and because so many large winners were caught, that it is now being so being so commented upon. It is doubtful that any legislation will ever wipe it out. For, what is privileged information ? Do not all experts trade on the fact that they know something that their client does not know ?

All of the Stock Exchange regulations are listed in a "Yellow

Book" and every journalist and adviser in financial matters needs to be fully aware of it, because the law does not take ignorance as an excuse.

Advance work is done through the media as a new company plans to go public. It is not a coincidence that a little-known company suddenly begins to get coverage on the business pages, that its previously anonymous chief executive and chairman suddenly become the material of profiles, that they are pictured at events and if they have a rags-to-riches story it is told over and over again. Then, as if out of the blue for the ordinary reader, that company announces that it is going public and will be raising money on the market. The planned entry of the giant GPA group to the world stock markets in 1992 was much-heralded and the notoriously media-shy executive chairman, Tony Ryan, suddenly became the person about whom every journalist wrote in the preceding months. Alas, the embarrassment was even greater when the flotation was aborted due to lack of interest with only 49 of the 85 million shares taken up.

If this advance work did not happen there would be less interest in the shares because nobody would know enough about the company to have trust in it. But it can backfire, as in the case of Xtravision. The video rental company was an overnight success. It rapidly expanded all over Ireland and into the UK and the US. It went public. Every paper was writing about it and about its owner Richard Murphy. The price soared. Then performance did not match up. The expansion had been too much too quick. Results were bad. The price dropped. Eventually, the leasing company, Cambridge, bought it out and restructured it.

Aggressive corporate advertising campaigns can also backfire. For instance, when Guinness and Argyle were fighting for control of Distillers, the slanging match through the pages of the quality press was particularly nasty. Hundreds of thousands of pounds were spent by each side abusing the other, at the end of which both companies suffered. The upshot was that whoever won, their credibility would be damaged amongst shareholders. The Stock Exchange has now banned such advertising.

Finance is a 24-hour activity and public relations has to respond. At every moment the markets somewhere in the world are busy. It is a frenetic, high-tension activity. Some would say it is only for young people. Massive salaries are earned by young men and women in the financial services area. But there is a high rate of burn out.

One interesting example of carefully-timed public relations was the collapse of Insurance Corporation of Ireland. It had only recently been taken over by Allied Irish Bank Group, but they found they had bought a disaster and that the potential underwriting losses were so massive that they could not even be measured. As banks need the confidence of their shareholders, AIB decided to close ICI and write off £90 million. But how were they to explain that to their shareholders ?

The issued a statement that they were getting out of ICI. But that meant the Government had to get involved because planes, ships, trains etc were all insured through ICI. So, the statement also declared that the bank was strong and would be paying its dividend. This seemed strange to the ordinary taxpayer with the Government seeming on one hand to have to repair the loss and then the cash-rich bank giving its shareholders a payout.

Further, the statement was issued on an Irish bank holiday when it was 9 am New York time, just as the money markets there were opening after the weekend. This timing was important because if there had been a loss of confidence in the bank AIB could have been refused lines of credit abroad and could even have been closed down through a run on its assets. And, that would have been an even greater worry for the Government.

ICI was rescued and re-structured without AIB and it is now wholly owned by AGF-Irish Life Holdings plc. The planes are still flying, the ships sailing and the trains rolling, and the taxpayer did not have to pay.

In the wheeling and dealing of the financial world, where scandals in all countries seem to be virtually hourly affairs, where people get fantastically rich very suddenly and display it in their lifestyle, can public relations remain pure ? Existing ethical codes were not framed with present knowledge of all the dealings that go on in the money world.

Some journalists feel that public relations people have lost their innocence through the close involvement with corporate finance. They are no longer the messengers just bringing in a press release written by their masters; they are right in on the decision-making and planning the strategy which is where they can be most effective. Some journalists feel this has cost them their objectivity and they are using their efforts to boost the share price rather than communicate fairly.

Journalists also resent the 'Friday night drop'. If there is bad news, Stock Exchange regulations are complied with by giving it in just on closing time on Friday before the markets can respond. Then it is dropped into the newspaper offices later that evening when the staff are tired and can't find anybody to comment. By opening time on Monday the bad news has been defused and the dreaded wobble in share price has probably been avoided. There is nothing openly unethical about this, but some see it as a sign that public relations is losing its sense of service to media. However, improved technology now makes it easier for the journalist to get it on her own screens without waiting for it to drop in.

Public relations advisers and journalists owe it to their professions to avoid any suspicion of unfair dealing. One British consultancy was very indignant when Government inspectors searched their offices after a leak involving a client; no wrongdoing was uncovered. A minimum precaution should be for no member of the public relations firm to hold shares in a client company.

Nor should journalists write about companies in which they have an interest, without declaring their position. *The Wall Street Journal* was greatly embarrassed when one of its columnists used his position to boost shares in which he had an interest and then sell before the truth was found out.

32.   Opinion leaders

TRADITIONALLY, journalists were the avenue to other audiences rather than an audience themselves; messengers, but not the final target.

Now, they set the agenda and influence the attitudes and opinions of their readers. The specialist journalist, often with academic qualifications and practical experience, is increasingly seen as an expert herself and more than a reporter of facts and of somebody else's opinions.

Specialist journalism developed in Ireland from the mid-sixties. The old reporter confined herself to facts and left the opinions to others in the formal editorial columns. Her journalism was anonymous. By-lines were rare; few readers even knew the name of the editor. Up to the 1960s, *The Times* of London never named its journalists; "The Times Correspondent", "Our Political Correspondent", "Our Own Correspondent", "A Correspondent" were the only attributions given.

Now journalists expect their by-lines on everything that they write. The specialist, be she in business, politics, finance, education, environment, arts or sport, is known and respected. Her views are sought and her readers expect more than the facts.

C.P.Scott, the old editor of the then Manchester Guardian,, said: "Comment is free; facts are sacred". But that does not happen in the new journalism. Facts and opinion are now so intertwined that they are at times inseparable. The value of the article is often judged by the credibility which the journalist has achieved. Whether this is a good or a bad trend, it is the reality and has consequences for anybody who needs to get messages to audiences and to influence their opinions and attitudes.

One must identify journalists and commentators who are relevant to one's business and ensure that they are properly informed. They need more than the press release, or the press reception to which many others are also invited; they have to be targeted for special briefings and individual attention.

These are the journalists to whom one speaks off the record knowing that trust will not be betrayed.

Writers, artists and musicians have always realised the importance of the critics. The critic is praised after a good review, but when it is bad, she is attacked as an ignorant person who counts for nothing. But the critics do count, even if they are not always as influential as in New York where a word from the senior theatre critic decides whether a show gets beyond its first night. Promoters, actors and theatre-owners wait in fear for the mighty critic's pen.

Rarely does the word of a political writer overthrow a government, although the investigative reporting of Robert Woodward and Carl Bernstein, two young journalists on *The Washington Post*, contributed to exposure of the Watergate scandal and the resignation of Richard Nixon. The power of the political writer is shown more in raising and articulating the issues which the public want but which the politicians are dodging. This is obvious at election time when the campaign opens to the government's agenda of issues, then switches to the opposition and ends up with the political writers and commentators.

Financial journalists can cause share prices to rise or fall; they can make or break a new issue. They write for an audience that is highly emotional and reactive to rumour. Just one word, especially from a writer who is respected as an objective observer, and they jump.

Beyond the special journalists are other opinion leaders - industrialists, politicians, trade unionists, academics, clerics, alickadoos[18] who seem to have constant access to the media. These are the people who do not mind being telephoned day or night for an instant quote. They may not all be experts but readers often believe them to be such.

For everything that happens there is an instant expert available to the media. The reporter on the story may not have special knowledge, or she may be in a hurry. This means she will lean on the 'expert'.

It is more difficult, but still possible to target these people. They should, like the special journalists, be identified as closely as possible, and given special attention.

Beyond journalists and media pundits are the wider field, the 'worthies', grey eminences who are respected in the highest circles. They may seldom be quoted in the media but they are consulted by those in high places; they are the opinion leaders, living in the virtually impenetrable inner circles, to whom the decision-makers really listen. Those who are relevant may be difficult to identify. The close confidantes of the Taoiseach usually get a nick-name, and are seen as a set, whether it be Donnybrook, Kinsealy or Country and Western.

They can include people of integrity like retired judges and civil servants - the sort of people government ministers ask to chair commissions of inquiry. The highest panel of worthies in the country is the President's Council of State whom she consults when, for instance, she is considering whether to sign a bill into law or refer it to the courts for judgement on its constitutionality.

How does one start to get a corporate message across to these opinion leaders ? Where does one stop ? Surely everybody is an opinion leader to those in her own circle. The public relations manager, or consultant, can help, acting as a sort of intelligence officer, feeding back what is really being said about the organisation, how it is really perceived and who is influencing the opinions and actions of others.

Says Jefkins of opinion leaders: "They may well be ignorant, hostile or prejudiced but certainly not apathetic. Or they could be knowledgeable, well-disposed or at least tolerant. Their attitudes can be dangerous or helpful, according to the extent of their knowledge and understanding".[19]

These experts, whether on taxation, consumer behaviour, aviation or earthquakes, need a constant flow of information. Never overlook them. Some of them might seem ignorant and boorish, but remember that those whom they influence are not always aware of this. Many of the gods have feet of clay when we meet them face-to-face but the public out there who admire them do not know this.

33. International

IRISH BUSINESS is being urged to think globally, not just Europe but worldwide - North and South America, Japan, Korea, China, Africa. Business people need to know how to compete and succeed in these markets. There is plenty of advice available on how to communicate across different cultures, preparing overseas markets for one's goods, and building a reputation abroad.

Kumi Sato, president of Cosmo Public Relations, in Tokyo, Japan says the practice of public relations is universal but the actual methods and strategies differ from country to country. Advising foreign companies trying to establish in Japan, she says one of their major problems is receiving advice from so many directions on how to do things in Japan.

"While companies entering the Japanese market must pay attention to customs and traditions in building relationships with Japanese staff, customers, clients and professional associates, I advise corporate executives new to Japan to follow their own business instincts and be creative in developing strategies for entering the Japanese market. Good business instincts are global and can be applied across the board".[20]

Communicating in home markets may not be easy, but penetrating a foreign market is an even greater challenge. For every McDonalds or Coca-Cola, there have been hundreds of failures, companies dipping into international markets and then pulling back. They often fail without realising, or admitting, that they have a communications problem.

The global trend in public relations is seen in the number of companies offering an international service through subsidiaries around the world. Among the international consultancies in Ireland are Hill & Knowlton, Ogilvy & Mather (through Wilson Hartnell), Edelman, Grayling, and Fleishman-Hillard.

For exporters and for international organisations, there is some advantage in dealing with public relations firms that are international. They have offices in the target countries and linkages as well as local knowledge. However, the quality of their work in Ireland is not a guarantee of the same in, say New York or Madrid or Tokyo.

Global public relations does not pose a threat for local professionals. As it is a business which deals with people, it always needs local knowledge. An Irish person in Tokyo would have difficulty dealing straight away with business people, staff, political leaders and journalists there. She could try, but her Japanese counterpart would have a running start on her.

The ways of business are different in each culture and those who want to succeed have to understand this. For instance, the Japanese can be frustrating for Westerners who are used to quick action and find it difficult to understand the Japanese way of conducting business through painstaking consensus.

The first problem in getting messages across internationally is translation. Will that brochure, press release, annual report, read properly in another language ? Probably not. More than the words will need translation. There is a whole new culture to understand.

Good homework is essential before stepping into the international market. Also, watch body language - a Japanese nodding her head up and down is not saying yes, but no. Know the audience and avoid condescension - the old colonial attitude is dead. Negotiating techniques vary. The French, for instance, like debate and argument and look at all the possible alternatives; the Japanese do not to haggle over price.

While the core task of communication is the same, methods of marketing and advertising differ greatly. One may decide to ignore these differences, not acceding to local cultures but going straight in convinced that one is right and there is only one right way to do anything. Few would imitate Luciano Benetton who puts the same advertisements into 92 countries. But then, these advertisements say nothing about the product (which is predominantly quality clothing) but are merely designed to shock people so much that they will look at the advertisements. It is easier to shock and annoy in 92 countries at one time than to please. Most of us want to please.

Another example of going against the tide was Avon cosmetics which in 1978 started an International Women's Running project to connect the name of Avon with beauty, health and fitness.[21] It fitted in with the company's international strategy, which was to promote greater opportunities for women at all levels in all societies.

The company set out to promote running in 20 countries, ranging from those where women's athletics was an established and respected sport to the less developed and less liberated countries of South America.

Brazil did not want to take part in the project, arguing to

headquarters that it was a very conservative country and had no tradition of women's running. They believed that the press would not cover such an event. Headquarters still felt the idea was good and adaptable in any market where Avon itself was a success. It went ahead with the race and by the fourth year more than 10,000 women took part in Brazil alone, and the press, because of the interest, were forced to cover it.

The key to this programme, which was standardised despite local differences, was not the status of women which was clearly not the same everywhere, but the worldwide trend towards an improvement in their status and the contribution, which Avon wanted to make.

International consultancies tend to specialise in areas which cross boundaries easier. For instance, Edelman sees three main areas where global reach can give their company the edge - financial, medical and technological. They feel that some other fields, such as consumer relations, are not yet as ready for such an international dimension. So far, most brands are not global but marketed for individual countries or groups of countries. There are lots of problems with, for instance, names and packaging and different tastes among consumers in different countries. There are few truly international products.

A typical task in an international consultancy, serving international clients, can be to run a campaign in several countries at one time. One Edelman example was a pan-European marketing campaign for a consortium of Japan's leading camera manufacturers. They had to plan and implement the campaign in 13 countries, dealing in Japanese and all of the other languages as well. They also had to co-ordinate five competing companies in each of the different markets. Then, they had to work with the International Red Cross and their totally autonomous organisations in the 13 countries in mounting a photographic competition which was the core of the campaign.

More than 18,000 entries had to be administered and judged over a 14-week period and Edelman were responsible for every detail including getting the 70 winners to Japan and back for their prize trip. David Davis, their former European manager described this as a "mammoth task which required military-style planning skills and an excessive amount of patience, tolerance and good-humour".[22]

On another typical occasion, Edelman had to organise a simultaneous press conference in New York and Brussels, linked by satellite, to announce an important development in the field of computer technology. They had eight working days to do it.

Notes

1   David Vevers, *Internal Communication*, in Pat Bowman (ed), *Handbook of Financial Public Relations*, Heinemann, Oxford, 1989, p. 35.

2   *Communication Briefings*, 140 South Broadway, Pitman, New Jersey 08071, Vol. 8 No. 2.

3   Feargal Quinn, *Crowning the Customer*, The O'Brien Press, Dublin, 1990, p. 130.

4   Lee Iacocca (with William Novak), *Iacocca - An Autobiography*, Sidgwick and Jackson, London, 1985. Several chapters consider this aspect of Iacocca's management style, especially chapters 5, 15 and 20.

5   cf. Seymour Hamilton, *A Communication Audit Handbook*, Pitman, London, 1987.

6   David Holden is director of public affairs with Bank of Ireland. As a consultant, first with Wilson Hartnell and then Holden Communications, he was involved in community and planning issues for major clients, including Asahi Ireland and Tara Mines. He was director of public affairs at Radio Telefís Eireann during the planning hearings about the mast for Atlantic 252 Radio in Co. Meath. He has spoken about community relations at courses and meetings organised by the Public Relations Institute of Ireland. See also, his article, *You and the Environment - the Role of PR*, Management, July 1977.

7   *The Irish Times*, 20 February 1990.

8   Thomas L. Harris, *The Marketer's Guide to Public Relations*, John Wiley & Sons, Inc., New York, 1991, ch. 11.

9   Communications Training plc, Garden Studios, 11-15 Betterton Street, Covent Gardens, London WC2H 9BP.

10   Marie Jennings, *Why the Customer is Always Right*, PR Week, 7 December 1989.

11   Frank Jefkins, *Public Relations Techniques*, Heinemann, London, 1988, p. 85.

12   cf. Nigel Ellis, *Parliamentary Lobbying*, Heinemann, Oxford, 1988. Report in PR Week, 22 September 1988, followed by review of the book by Bob Cryor, MP, PR Week, 29 September 1988.

13   Originally delivered in lecture to Public Relations Institute of Ireland, Dublin, 26 January 1982. Subsequently developed in *Marketing Opinion* and in lectures to Rathmines and PRII students. See also Myles Tierney, *The Parish Pump*, Able Press, Dublin, 1982.

14   Oliver Donohue, Irish Congress of Trade Unions, to meeting of Public Relations Institute of Ireland, 15 November 1988.

15   Ted Nealon, TD, same PRII meeting.

16   Katie Arber, *The Practice of Public Relations*, Traverse-Healy & Regester Ltd, London, 1986 (Thesis for M.Sc in Management Studies).

17   cf. Paul Holmes, *A Problem for the High Flyers*, PR Week, 30 April 1987.

18   Dictionaries do not define an alickadoo, but to this writer he is the hurler-on-the-ditch, the man at the football match or on the bar stool who has all the answers and can recall every move of the game and why so-and-so did not score and what the referee should have done for this or for that. One Holy Ghost priest. the late Walter Finn, used it as his by-line for an occasional column in *The Irish Independent*.. The same "Wally" Finn was a rugby football trainer of brilliance and would be highly valued if he were alive to-day !

19   Frank Jefkins, *Public Relations Techniques*, Heinemann, London, 1988, p. 86.

20   *An Interview with International PR Expert, Kumi Sato*, Communication World, IABC, June 1988.

21   cf. Frank Ovatt,Jr. in paper, *Communicating in Worldwide Markets*, to IPRA/Public Relations Society of America conference, 1987.

22   David Davis, then Edelman's general manager, Europe, in lecture to Public Relations Institute of Ireland certificate course, 15 March 1989.

<u>Chapter Four</u>

Why Public Relations is Really Necessary: The Playing Fields

Public relations is relevant on every playing field, throughout the whole of life and business, because everything that an organisation says or does has a public relations consequence. This chapter selects a few of these playing fields and considers some of the issues on each of them. In responding to the issues public relations will not always play in the same position. It might be a forward with a high profile; or in mid-field with a strong supporting role; or in defence, seeking to create opportunity from adversity; or in goal, taking shots from all directions and primarily intent on keeping the ball out of the net.The reader is invited to add to these issues and to describe other playing fields with the best positions for public relations.

34.   Arts & Culture

"All our literature and art are for the masses of the people, and in the first place for the workers, peasants and soldiers; they are created for the workers, peasants and soldiers and are for their use" -
Mao Tse-Tung[1]

ARTISTS, writers and musicians need help to survive because, on their own, they tend to be unbusiness-like. Art, as used here, covers all forms of art - painting, sculpture, literature, drama, music.

Public relations for arts and culture must reach beyond the elite, in addition to embracing sponsorship and event management. Filling seats is vital, but a climate of awareness and acceptance has to be created first.

Beyond the elite
Those who pursue and follow the arts tend to be a small group, mixed as to culture and experience. It is a mistake to see them as an elite or special. The arts are neither morally good nor bad and one is not necessarily a better or a worse person for being interested or not in them.

"There has never been anything immaculate about the conception of art. The very notion that there ought to be is itself socially conditioned by developments peculiar to the last century.....Art is as much a part of the social framework as any other process of production. There is nothing ethereal about the artist. He does a job like anyone else", says Ciaran Carty[2].

Public relations can help to recapture the arts from the elite. Those outside the inner circle must be shown that there are no barriers, that art, music and literature are for everybody to experience and enjoy.

Education through the schools and the community is one strategy. Publications, talks, visits to galleries and concerts, competitions and projects can show the way.

Artists like Robert Ballagh realise that art is for all and they give practical expression to it by bringing it into the community.

During the renovation of the Custom House in Dublin, he organised the local children to paint a giant mural along the builders' hoardings.

The phoney approach to the arts should be crushed, along with the mystique that nobody else can possibly understand or appreciate the real meaning of art. In some cases, perhaps, the creator intended no meaning beyond painting a picture or telling a story. James Joyce, Flann O'Brien, Paddy Kavanagh and others would be ribald in ridicule at the industries which have grown up around their works.

More people know about Pavarotti than probably any other classical musician, helped to an extent by the 1990 World Cup in Italy. But among the elite, there is a suggestion that this is cheapening the art. Likewise they scoff at the piano-playing of Richard Cledermann. Of course, he lacks musical technique, but he never claimed to be a top concert performer. He found a niche and through his gentle medleys brought the classical composers to millions who would never sit through a symphony concert.

Opera suffers a lot from its elite, but the town of Wexford has shown, for more than 40 years, that even with the dress-suits, bow-ties and the strange language, it can be something for the whole community to enjoy.

It is not easy to give art back to the multitude. As Ciaran Carty says: "The whole elitist notion of 'art' being by the few for the few - an exercise in form without reference to time and place - has nurtured the phenomenal growth of the international art market in the twentieth century: there is a vested interest in its continued currency. Some indication of the scale of this market is the fact that Sothebys and Christies alone netted over £350,000,000 auctioning art in 1979"[3].

Sponsorship

The arts need money, and traditionally they have been assisted by wealthy patrons. Nowadays business has replaced the popes, kings and princes of old. But it is unreasonable to see the money as a pure gift to be used without accountability. In accepting a sponsor one accepts certain conditions. It is a mutually beneficial arrangement, with give and take on both sides.

The formation of Cothú - the Business Council for the Arts - has encouraged sponsorship in a practical sense by acting as a broker to bring the artist and the sponsor together.

However, a good case has to be made to the sponsor because there is a lot of competition. The numbers pursuing the arts will always be greater than the market seeking them. A professional, written presentation must outline the amount required and what will be done with it, as well as how much will be raised from other sources. The benefits to the sponsor must be set out in detail, giving also an idea of how efficient the organisation is. Even the most altruistic sponsor will not give money if it is going to be wasted by well-meaning but disorganised recipients.

Event management

The arts need events and there must be somebody to organise them. Artists should be allowed get on with their art rather than worry about organising the details of the exhibition or the concert. There are many events competing for attention and only a limited number of people with the leisure time to patronise them.

Public relations has to work with marketing and promotions to make these events special. There is scope for imagination and it does not have to be inward-looking. Some of the best events have looked outward, raising money for those in need. The Live Aid concert, organised by Bob Geldof in 1985, did a lot to bring popular music to those who previously dismissed it as juvenile delinquency.

It is hard work organising a concert or an art show and one does not always have time to sit back and define the barriers between management disciplines. It is a mixture of public relations, marketing, advertising and promotion. There are constant checklists - venues, posters, press notices, programmes, ticket distribution, merchandising items, news angles, photocalls, facilities for journalists to meet performers, traffic and security arrangements on the day, publicity follow-up and so on.

The arts do not have to be beggars. With proper business organisation, the product can be brought to the market, with ever-wider audiences identified and made aware, so that everybody can have fun, for art is essentially an activity to be enjoyed. The product can be good, but the customer will be frightened if she finds a guard of eunuchs at the door, holding her back from a holy of holies and scorning her uncouth interest.

35. Charities

"But I have reservations about portraying this country (Ethiopia), where what strikes you immediately is the people's dignity not their poverty, as a land of passive victims who cannot help themselves when in fact if you give them the means they work incredibly hard and strive to look after themselves" - Edith Simmons, UNICEF[4]

THERE ARE an unknown number of charities in Ireland raising a sum that is also unknown, but estimated at anything from £20 to £100 million. They use every publicity technique to make known their causes and encourage people to support them. This includes advertising, exhibitions, lectures, literature, events, celebrity endorsements and stunts.

The most obvious public relations issues for Irish charities are credibility, respect for the victims and fundraising.

Credibility

There is little supervision of charities; nobody knows how much many of them collect nor how much goes to the stated causes. They rely a lot on voluntary help and that is always well-intentioned but often unprofessional, unskilled and wasteful of resources.

The competition between charities is great, such that they scandalise at times by the uncharitable way in which they deal towards one another. For example, a libel action brought by World Vision of Ireland against Trócaire, the Catholic Third World relief organisation, got as far as the High Court in Dublin where it was struck out by consent.

K

Bureaucracy can scandalise, as when charities do not wish to offend governments in the stricken countries and when procedural wrangles stop the distribution of the aid which has been given. Concern, originally the Joint Biafra Famine Appeal when it was set up in 1968, arose from frustration at the difficulties which the Irish Red Cross was having at getting the aid into the country.

The public relations approach to each charity has to be different but all need to state honestly what they do with their funds if they are to have credibility. The 'unique selling point' for the Society of St. Vincent de Paul, which raises about £8 million a year in Ireland, is that every penny goes to the poor. None of its workers are paid, contributing instead themselves to a separate fund to pay for expenses.

Respect for the victims

Charities, in their desire to shock people into giving, can overlook the importance of the victims' dignity. Shock tactics create an immediate reaction, but in the long term they can be counterproductive and very bad public relations.

Each year there is a protest by disabled people at the filming of ITV's *Telethon* which raises more than £20 million for charity, about a quarter of which goes to disabled people. The leader of the protest, known as Block Telethon, is Alan Holdsworth, a musician and a poet. He also blocks BBC's *Children in Need* fundraiser. This year there were 1,000 disabled people outside the London Weekend Television studios for the *Telethon* protest. Their concern is that the programme portrays them as objects of charity and as helpless, able to survive only thanks to the philanthropy of the able-bodied. They feel the appeal, by reinforcing negative preconceptions about the disabled, does more harm than good. They would prefer that able-bodied people be encouraged to make them members of their pubs and clubs, employ them, let them into their schools, give them reasonable access to public places. They say they need that more than the donations which, though welcome, will never solve their problems.

What picture do charities as a whole present of the Third World? To most people it is one of communities stricken by disaster, unable to take care of themselves. That is the picture which inspires people to help now. But there is little of the positive side of life in these countries shown, because that would not pull upon the purse strings to the same extent. There is little seen of the immense efforts the people themselves have made to overcome their problems. The human dignity of the sufferers is not taken into account. The naked, starving person in a famine camp, with flesh hanging from the bones and flies crawling all over, is still a person with dignity.

Publicity material from charities too often emphasises the negative side, the problems, and shows less of the industrial and agricultural progress, the new cities, the schools and the universities. Governments are usually portrayed as not caring, inept and corrupt. There is corruption in the Third World and it is strange when people in one country, with its own poverty, are asked to alleviate problems in another country where governments and authorities maintain the trappings of power and a luxurious lifestyle. It has to be remembered that the ordinary starving people are the victims, not the supporters, of these corrupt governments.

Says Edith Simmons: "When you live here (Ethiopia), as I do, you see very clearly that there are no straightforward villains, that no sudden change of regime would change the fundamental fate of the people"[5].

Fundraising

The skills of public relations are not strictly speaking those of fundraising, but in a charity, whether it be for illness and poverty at home, or for underdevelopment and natural disaster abroad, everybody concerned has to think of fundraising.

Public relations can develop new ways of bringing the issues to the attention of the public as well as assessing their wider implications. Not everybody is going to help every charity; everybody has their own special causes, often because of a personal experience or of some tragedy which has struck close to them.

Stephen Farrelly, director of communications and fundraising at the Rehabilitation Institute, says that charities are now coming under pressure to provide "a bang for a buck" as they compete with the National Lottery for consumers' discretionary income. "If you're out collecting with just a can you can forget it", he says[6].

The flag has been an old gimmick, helping to advertise the charity further and saving contributors from being pestered by every other collector in town. But new and imaginative ideas had to be sought. The Irish Cancer Society have their annual Daffodil Day, an idea copied by others who give such things as roses, apples and santa claus hats.

Special groups, also, have called upon their peers. The immense success of Bob Geldof with Live Aid showed the generosity of the people in the music world. Likewise John O'Shea, through GOAL, has brought in Irish and international sportspeople to his work. But all of these realise that the work does not stop when the money is given; it has to be seen to be given to the people who need it.

There was debate a few years ago in Britain before ITV allowed charities to advertise. It was feared that those with the biggest purses would win and the smaller groups would lose. However, in the first two and half years of advertising, less than 40 charities have done so. It has helped awareness but not done as much as expected for fund-raising.

This is not surprising, as advertising research had already shown that only 5 % respond to direct advertisements for donations. Personal request is the favourite method of giving and that is where the more subtle approach of public relations helps.

36. Civil Service

"The traditional attitude has been to present as narrow a front as possible towards the public, since from that direction there is little to be expected except mud and brickbats. Consequently, information is strictly controlled or channelled - sometimes to the point of ceasing to flow at all" - Desmond Roche[7].

MUCH HAS changed since Roche was writing in 1963. Then, the civil servants in the Government Information Bureau went home at 5 pm and refused media calls after that time. In 1973, the Bureau became the Government Information Service, and it employed professional journalists and public relations people. Now each department also has its own information officer who is allowed considerable discretion.

Emphasis in civil service public relations should be on finding out if the old stereotypes are still true, and, if so, countering them; in corporate identity; and in efficient media relations and presentation of information about policies, entitlements and services.

Killing the stereotype

Negative stereotypes have hounded the civil service - faceless, cautious, secretive, unimaginative, paper-pushers, and so on. But the reality is now changing. Promotion is now on merit. Heads of departments are appointed for fixed terms. Service to the public is more personal. There is greater mobility of staff, with fixed-term appointments, transfer between departments, recruitment from outside professional and commercial life. Following the 1969 publication of the Report of the Public Services Organisation Review Group, better known as the Devlin Report, the distinction has been increasingly made between the policy-making and the executive roles in the civil service. But do public perceptions change as readily ?

Civil servants are cautious because, while ministers come and go, they remain to pick up the pieces when mistakes are made. Core policy cannot afford to change with every minister.

The minister, personifying her department, takes responsibility for everything. Selfless, rather than anonymous, civil servants have been happy to frame policy and let the minister make it her own and take the credit for it. These people are part of a structure which has been incorruptible and totally loyal to successive governments. However, a more educated public now demands to know who they are and how they have arrived at their decisions.

Stereotyping can be lessened by allowing civil servants who take the decisions to be identified, and doing away with the fiction that the minister decides everything. Managing directors of large companies do not pretend to do everything themselves; they work with strong management teams. Civil servants should not be any different. When ministers are fighting for funds at the cabinet table, more often than not the effective lobbying has been done between their respective civil servants.

Corporate identity

Like any other organisation, the civil service has physical characteristics which are its corporate identity. If it pays attention to them and co-ordinates them it can present itself as coherent, confident and efficient. If it neglects them, people, regardless of performance, will remain hooked to the old, damaging stereotypes and both morale and recruitment will suffer.

The corporate identity of the Irish civil service has changed constantly since 1922, but its presentation has not always reflected this. Civil service offices, even those which have dealings with the public, have often been the most drab. Is this a true reflection of the reality, or mere carelessness ?

Letterheads are needed anyway, so why not design a strong, attractive style with a distinctive logo instead of the same old stuff as has been sent out for the past seventy years. The corporate personality should not be one of anonymity.

Media relations and public information

The Devlin Report referred to the absence of effective communication and dialogue between the public service and the community. The administrative system in Ireland has always tended more towards keeping information from journalists. Civil servants have not been accustomed to open discussion on matters of public concern. They have had to obtain permission to publish or to appear on radio or television, and, "in practice, have often found it quite hard to get it, even for innocuous material. Such activities have not been encouraged, to say the least"[8].

The services offered by the department are its products and they have to be packaged and presented with the same skill as any other product. They have to be attractively presented and explained in language which the public can understand. But, the Official Secrets Act forbids a civil servant to tell any outsider what happens in the department or what she learns at her work. As long as that act stands, it will require considerable flexibility for a department to tell anybody anything properly.

For instance, the Department of Social Welfare, with its complex web of services, is constantly on call for radio chat shows and phone-ins. It requires great skill to be a credible spokesperson, answering questions without breaching confidentiality and explaining complex regulations in a few seconds.

Increasing demands by the media mean an increasing number of civil servants are being trained professionally. Quite a few have completed the certificate course of the Public Relations Institute of Ireland.

The tools of public relations are essentially the same in the civil service as in any corporation, conscious and aware of its communication needs. They include press conferences, reports, newsletters, public meetings, speeches, exhibitions, advertising and so on. One progressive example has been the Revenue Commissioners. In recent years, they have included poster advertising to tell the employers and the public about tax amnesties, self-assessment and the need to get important company documents submitted in time.

37. Defence Forces

"Communications affecting the Defence Forces generally or any arm or branch of the Service that it may be desirable to make to the Press, will normally issue from An Runaí, Roinn Cosanta (Secretary, Department of Defence). The preparation of all such communications will normally be the duty of the Director of Intelligence. When accredited Press representatives are granted permission to visit Army establishments, or accompany a force in the field (e.g. during training or manoeuvres), they will be controlled by the Director of Intelligence" - *Defence Forces regulations 29 (1)[9] .*

THE REGULAR defence forces of 13,000 include the Army, the Air Corps and the Navy. Traditionally, public relations for them has not been high on the national agenda. They are usually overlooked in writings and discussions on the government and administration of Ireland, surprising in view of the emotive attention paid to neutrality.

However, they now have a higher profile and a greater need to communicate. It started with the first United Nations peace-keeping missions from 1958 and developed with the involvement in Border security from 1968.

The Gleeson Report into working conditions and organisational structures recommended increased attention to public relations and an expanded press office. This has now been implemented with co-ordination of all communications functions and direct access for public relations to the Chief of Staff.

Key issues for the Defence Forces include media relations, internal communication and the recruitment of good personnel.

Media Relations

The Defence Forces need to explain what they are doing as well as react to media enquiries. National security will always require a discretion that might not be as important on other playing fields, but the new post-Gleeson openness should in the future reduce the amount of misinformed comment and negative perceptions.

Spokespeople for the defence forces need to be confident, credible and of sufficient rank to carry authority. They need to be trained and to have clear lines of authority so that they know what they are permitted to say.

However, the tension between the professional military Defence Forces and the civilian Department of Defence is always a factor to remember. Members of the public will not always be clear as to how responsibility for issues is apportioned.

The UN experience has often turned to tragedy with 70 lives lost since the Niemba ambush in the Congo in 1961. Communication with bereaved families is also important, but some relatives have criticised the lack of follow-up and years later they still have nothing but the barest details about how their husbands or sons were killed.

The public have a lot of goodwill for the defence forces. RTE assists with requests programmes and sends interviewers to the UN missions at times like Christmas and St. Patrick's Day. Singers have been brought out to entertain the troops, but surprisingly this initiative started with British Airways flying Geraldine Branigan to Cyprus.

Internal communication

Unrest in the Defence Forces increased through the 1980s, exposing cumbersome administrative structures and inadequate means of internal communication. It took a long time for the authorities to accept there was a problem.

The Forces are easily taken for granted. Send them to the UN, bring them out when the buses go on strike, send them to the Border, but forget that they are family people and that their pay and conditions have at times been appalling. Also, they have been frustrated in their professional duties through cutbacks which have deprived them of resources. Once upon a time, there was even a cruel joke going the rounds that they had not live ammunition for their training exercises and had to shout "bang, bang" !

They cannot go on strike and they used not have any means of raising grievances. They were not allowed to have internal representative bodies until 1989 following an extensive lobbying campaign by their spouses. It got national coverage and some wives even ran at the general election, worrying the Government greatly because a country at peace can too easily take its loyal troops for granted.

Recruitment

In times of high unemployment there should not be any problem gaining recruits for an exciting and secure area like the Defence Forces. But, the calibre of recruit is what matters.

The attractions of the career are presented to young men and women and open days are held at barracks throughout the country. It is shown as a good career, and a secure job, with promotion open to all on merit. An unexpected bonus came through the university television quiz, *Challenging Times*, in which the Cadet School of the Curragh Military College reached the semi-final in 1992 and showed the country how bright they were[10].

Television and press have been used to show the excitement of the life with shots from training exercises to appeal to adventurous young people. But there can always be a danger of over-glamourising these situations. For instance, some extended advertisements featured the Army Ranger Wing, an SAS-type unit which prides itself on superior fitness, team spirit, military skills and flexibility in all operations. Not all recruits are suitable for such high-class service.

The prospect of action with the UN is an attraction, but it must be portrayed honestly. War is never pleasant, even for the peacekeepers, and soldiers' conditions can be grim and nerve-shattering, made tolerable only by the financial rewards. Some have criticised the muted welcome which they received on returning home after such service.

38.   Fashion

"It's not a booming industry, but it has great potential that's not being tapped. It needs to be promoted in the same way as the food industry promotes its brands and Ireland should strive to be seen as a quality supplier of designer clothes". - Reg McCabe, Confederation of Irish Industry[11].

THE IRISH fashion industry employs 10,000 people and has a turnover of more than £700 million a year. It covers designers, manufacturers and retailers of clothes as well as beauty products.

Public relations for this industry is too often seen merely as marketing support; for real public relations to emerge it has to go further and become independent of both marketing and advertising. Public relations has to respond to the great environmental and ethical issues as well as looking after media relations and enhancement of the market.

Social responsibility

The fashion industry is facing a growing crisis which could engulf it, with accusations of exploiting women, being cruel to animals, destroying the environment and being dishonest with its customers. The immensely successful Body Shop, a revolution in the manufacture and selling of beauty products, and now almost worldwide, has never had a marketing department nor spent a penny on advertising. Its success has been built on real public relations - having a social conscience, using natural products and giving honest information to customers.

"I hate the beauty business", writes Anita Roddick who, with her husband, Gordon, opened the first Body Shop at Brighton in 1976. "It is a monster industry selling unattainable dreams. It lies. It cheats. It exploits women. Its major product lines are packaging and garbage. It is no wonder that Elizabeth Arden once said that the cosmetics business was the 'nastiest in the world"[12] .

The industry has to face this crisis and the new public awareness. Otherwise it will not survive. Public relations has to be its conscience, pushing it to behave itself, and trying to prevent customers being given dishonest information and impossible dreams. It has to be a strong and separate voice to top management, because its advice will not always be what the marketing people want to hear.

Roddick, travelling all over the world, kept finding examples of women using local natural ingredients for skin and hair care. "It was a revelation to realise that there were women all over the world caring for their bodies perfectly well without ever buying a single cosmetic. These women were doing exactly what we were doing in the west in the way of polishing, protecting and cleansing their skin and hair, but they were doing it with traditional natural substances instead of formulated ingredients".[13]

Media relations

Journalistic respect for public relations in fashion has grown since the days described by one London consultant: "Leeches and pirhanas. That's how we were seen. We were sometimes treated by the companies that hired us, as the enemy. They retained. They didn't respect. They didn't understand public relations. They did not know how to use it. They used to take us on because it was an egotistical thing to do. It was very upsetting"[14] .

Fashion designers rely heavily on large, glitzy events to show their products. These events, often linked with charities, do not necessarily lead to sales, but are exercises in creating awareness. In practice, the role of public relations tends to be looking after the press rather than organising the details of the event.

There are about ten shows, twice a year, featuring top Irish designers. But there are trends elsewhere to show that this may be changing. Two of France's fashion houses, Thierry Mugler and Kenzo, withdrew from the 1992 spring shows in Paris. A suggested reason was that "designers recognise that their shows have become a media circus, a fashion version of the Cannes Film Festival. They say the show season no longer has any relevance to the business of selling clothes: orders for 70 % of sales are wrapped up at least a fortnight before the shows take place"[15].

Expense cannot be spared at fashion shows. Only the best models and the best photography will succeed. No designer will get anywhere with holiday snapshot presentations. The full press launch of a clothes collection in Dublin can cost as much as £10,000, with model and production costs at £3,000, photography £2,000 and £5,000 on hospitality, champagne and lunch[16].

There is no shortage of good news stories in fashion. The journalist values good public relations because the industry worldwide is so complex that it helps to have somebody up-to-date and able to decode the latest ideas and trends. Everybody wears clothes and to some extent uses beauty products and nearly everybody is interested in the fashion world even if to the minimal extent of having views on whether hemlines should go up or down.

The journalists know that the priority is to sell the clothes and cosmetic products, but they also know that their readers like to read about these subjects, even if the borderline between puffery and objective news is finer than in other areas of journalism.

This does not mean that quality can be any less. Any journalist knows when she is being spoofed. If the product is good and the customer is getting genuine value the journalist will not be inhibited in writing about it.

Lynne Franks, a doyenne of the British fashion public relations for more than 20 years, says: "I have seen too many consultancies promise the client the moon to win the account, and then of course, they can't deliver. That is the way not only to lose business, but to lose credibility. You also have to realise exactly what journalists want, and then give them it"[17].

Enhancement

It would be impossible to estimate the good that President Mary Robinson is doing for Irish fashion worldwide. She always wears Irish clothes from up-and-coming as well as top labels. She has made a tremendous impression in the United States, France and elsewhere with added amazement when it is realised that all of her clothes are Irish. She has been nominated as one of the best dressed women in the world. An ambassador of such stature and popularity is an unprecedented opportunity for Irish fashion. Such endorsement is worth more than any advertising campaign.

Buying and wearing Irish has still a long way to go, even at home. Less than a quarter of Irish fashion purchases are on Irish-made products, despite the high reputation for quality that Irish designers have been achieving for many years. It is an area of special effort to change this and promote the benefits of buying Irish.

Customers have been conditioned to the quality reputation of continental labels, turning down an Irish product that may be superior merely because they are convinced that the French or Italian label is better. The worldwide merchandising of Gucci products, for instance, shows the value of a branded quality name. The aura has rubbed off on to a whole range of products, even as far as keyrings.

Many are convinced that there is quality in Irish fashion, but, as Carol Flynn points out, that conviction has not spread to spending money. The EC offers generous grants for marketing but the Irish fashion industry has not been able to take them all up because it is not prepared to raise one third of the money itself[18].

39.   Gaelic Athletic Association

"Terrified to face the sectarian and bigoted elements within its own identity, the GAA takes refuge in a fog of official-speak...." Fintan O'Toole.[19]

NATIONALIST politics and Gaelic language and culture have been integral to the Gaelic Athletic Association (GAA) since its foundation in 1884; the games of hurling, gaelic football and camogie are merely outward expressions of this one form of Irishness.

The first priority for the GAA to-day is the promotion and support of its games and it achieves this with tremendous efficiency, but it faces important issues in public relations, including its identity, local misunderstandings, and sponsorship.

A question of identity

The GAA doesn't want to abandon its nationalist traditions, but likewise it doesn't know whether it should defend and explain them. It has a historic identity but needs to decide what its identity should be today and to present it unambiguously.

The ban on GAA members playing or attending 'foreign games' ended in 1971. Foreign sports were those which had their origin in England. However, the ban mentality has lived on and has been reinforced by the past 20 years of unrest in Northern Ireland. The GAA is identified with the nationalist minority. Northern police and soldiers, and their families, are still barred from membership.

In 1991 the GAA refused permission for a double-bill at the RDS, Dublin, with a soccer game preceding a fundraising gaelic football game. Arguments about grounds not being vested in the GAA, and anxiety as to how the funds would be distributed, were given as reasons for forbidding the game, for which approval had originally been granted at a lower level in the organisation. They allowed the crisis and the criticism to build up, then took a decision, but at first refused spokesmen to explain it, leaving all the best points to be made by their opponents. When they did explain themselves, it was too late; their credibility had been over-stretched. Many had welcomed the fixture as a symbol of the GAA burying its sectarian past, but the administrators decided to bury the present to the great distress of many of their members and the general public. For veteran GAA writer Paddy Downey, it "was the blackest day in the long and chequered history of the association"[20].

The GAA seems to react excitedly when soccer is mentioned, but has no hesitation in allowing Croke Park to be used for American football, for boxing, or for foreign pop music concerts. Some contradiction somewhere, which even led to its patron, Archbishop Dermot Clifford of Cashel, asking that there be no repeat of the Féile concerts in the GAA Semple Stadium in Thurles. He complained of riotous behaviour and underage drinking. "Any sporting event in Semple Stadium is infinitely preferable to the Féile", he said[21]. There is now a massive redevelopment of Croke Park under way, an ideal opportunity for all of Irish sport to have a stadium of international prestige, but the GAA is still determined not to involve other sporting bodies, knowing that it can raise all of the money needed without any help.

Local misunderstandings

The GAA has a magnificent product. It commands massive support throughout Ireland with 800,000 members and 306,000 players in more than 2,000 clubs with 20,000 teams. Its games remain very attractive to young people and traditional county and club clashes inspire undying loyalty.

However, there sometimes seems to be two GAAs - official GAA and the GAA of the ordinary players and public at large. They certainly do not seem to agree on what the GAA should be. This is seen on such occasions as the ban on the RDS game, which raised protest from many players, past and present, including former Taoiseach, Jack Lynch, one of the most distinguished and successful players ever on a GAA field.

For journalist Sean Kilfeather: "The GAA tends to be secretive about its business and often prefers to conceal matters of interest to the public rather than revealing them. This doesn't only refer to matters of controversy which might be seen as not reflecting all that favourably on the association. The hierarchy also tends to run for cover whenever anything comes up which might be of interest in a general way."

Kilfeather wants the GAA to adopt a more open door approach to "things which happen in the corridors of power which are quite properly of interest to the rank and file of the members of the association and to the general public"[22].

As with the government and the Roman Catholic Church, the whole country takes an interest in GAA issues and ignorance is no obstacle to punditry. One of them is dirty play which is not exclusive to the GAA but inevitable in all games of physical contact. When journalists raise the question, often with a greater shock than they would for rugby or soccer, official GAA rushes onto the defensive and attacks the media for telling lies.

GAA public relations officer, Danny Lynch, would not deny there is dirty play. He says the media are generally fair in their treatment of the issue. "But I would reckon that perhaps the specialist journalists in other sports are not as fair in the sense that if there's an incident in a GAA game it suddenly becomes national news. If there's an incident in some other sports that I could mention, it's rarely referred to and it becomes 'ungentlemanly conduct' or 'over-robust play"[23].

Attitudes to sponsorship

The GAA is a great attraction for sponsors and many deals have been negotiated at club and county levels. The first big sponsorship was of the All-Stars and their trips to New York, introduced in the 1970s by Carrolls. It was costing Carrolls £30,000 a year and despite pressure from then Health Minister, Charles Haughey and prominent GAA priest, Leo Morahan, that it was wrong to take sponsorship from a cigarette company, the advice "went in one ear and out the other". Finally, Carrolls dropped it in 1979 and it was taken over by Bank of Ireland. Seán O Síocháin, then retiring as director-general of the GAA but given the job to raise funds for a new headquarters at Croke Park, approached Carroll's public relations manager, Pat Heneghan, and persuaded him to give the £30,000 that year for the development.[24]

The GAA is now going for the jackpot and seeking sponsors for the All-Ireland hurling and football championships. These will be the most prestigious sponsorships in Irish sport, and the price initially sought, unsuccessfully, was between £1.5 and £2 million a year over three years, described by the GAA as "Europe's last great sponsorship opportunity". It did not go ahead as planned in 1992 because, it is believed, the potential sponsors, believed to include a bank, a brewery, a car manufacturer and two semi-state companies, were making too many demands.

In a move which shocked many stalwarts of the Association, it spoke to would-be sponsors about "tailoring the presentation of the championship to suit your company's objectives" and referred to "your All-Ireland championship"[25].

The national leagues are already sponsored and have not been free of controversy. In 1984, Fords closed their motor factory in Cork with heavy redundancies. The general perception was that they behaved badly to the community which had been loyal to them. They then rushed into a succession of sponsorships of cultural and sporting events. Many organisations welcomed them, principally the GAA, with a special centenary tournament and then the sponsorship of the national leagues. This got the Ford good name back into every parish of the country. Ford management afterwards admitted it was cynical, but as far as they were concerned, it worked, silencing the reaction to the closure.[26]

When Ford's cosmetic job was done, they dropped the sponsorship. The GAA then turned to the British-owned Royal Liver insurance company, an anomalous choice in some ways, given the traditions of the GAA.

40.   Garda Siochana

"Even when the Civic Guard was founded (1922), what with such a backlog of goodwill to recapture, the need for a publicity bureau must have been self-evident. In those days, the nearest the force ever got to a publicity officer was the composer of that naive and rakish porter shark, 'Are you there, Mory-ar-i-tee ?', a ballad which grabbed the Irish imagination as much as 'The daughter of Officer Kelly' grabbed the Irish-American sense of romance".[27]

THE GARDA SIOCHANA are aware of the importance of professional public relations, but it has been difficult for them to "leap from the era of tight-lipped secrecy to the more open attitudes of modern life"[28].

The central public relations issues for the garda include their role as the protectors of the people, media relations and community relations.

Protecting the people

Garda Siochana means Guardians of the Peace. The public always address them as 'guard', never as 'officer', and talk about the 'guards', not the 'police'. Every member of the 11,000 strong force is a public relations person in both public and private life.

In Ireland, the public see the unarmed gardaí as their protectors against the criminal. It is not the same elsewhere. In China, for instance, a young policeman admitted to David Rice that his role was to protect the government against the citizen[29].

In presenting themselves as the people's protectors it can be difficult for the gardaí because they have unpopular powers which they have to use - to stop, search, arrest and detain. They often meet people when people do not want to meet them - at the commission of an offence, in the delivery of a summons, after an arrest, or when they are the bearers of bad news after an accident.

As they are guardians of the peace, people too easily blame them when the peace has been disturbed. They have to shoulder the blame for everybody else in society. They can be hit suddenly by a crisis which is not of their making - a murder, a robbery, a kidnap, a prison escape. Within minutes they are the focus of nationwide media attention and the local superintendent is being asked - what has happened, why did it happen, what are you going to do about it? But, she cannot blame, she has to be the ultimate diplomat. It is not her fault that the banks failed in their security and allowed robbers to walk out in broad daylight with £2 million.

In addition to the sudden crises they have to be tuned to those which start as problems and recur, often building up to a media high point if they are not handled early - attacks on old people, muggings in city streets, car thefts and 'joy-riding', drugs, and so on.

People blame the police for crime. But, gardaí do not commit the crimes, nor do they create the social conditions in which crime flourishes, nor do they pass sentence, nor do they let prisoners out. They do their best to prevent crime and to detect it when it happens, but they are far from being the only players on the field.

The yearly crime figures are interpreted as an annual report on the garda activity and this is a public relations issue about which something could be done. The Department of Justice controls the presentation of these figures, even though they are issued through the Garda Commissioner's office. They are riddled with opportunity for misrepresentation.

Media relations

A police force needs active as well as reactive media relations. Morale within the force, as well as the public interest, requires an efficient channel for it to explain itself. If such a channel is not developed, the impression will be given of a force that is "slow, ponderous and suspicious"[30]. Seamus Breathnach wrote nearly twenty years ago that "practically every police writer throughout the world will readily admit that ever since the constable was allotted his bailiewick he has been given a bad press"[31].

Gardaí have been concerned that not enough has been done to give them a better press. "The sharpest criticism of the Garda's public relations operation has come from within the ranks and members have not been reluctant to voice their opinions at conference time"[32].

Police work can be very frustrating. Criminals are detected, arrested and convicted but then often released immediately on to the streets to continue their crimes because there are no jails for them. Then, people wonder why the gardaí are not 'doing something' about, say, car theft, drugs, burglaries. Also, criminals and concerned groups are quick to accuse the gardaí of ill-treatment, even when there is no basis for the claim.

The gardaí, therefore, must have an opportunity to explain themselves and defend their integrity. But, 'rotten apples' who are found to act improperly must be seen to be properly disciplined.

Florida police commissioner William A Liquori, emphasises the need for an open attitude in police/press relations. "We as professionals must accept the media's right to review our actions. We must take stands on issues, be willing to state things publicly and be ready to defend our statements. These actions must be taken effectively and in a professional manner".[33]

"In dealing with the media, two questions arise, how much can the gardaí reveal and how much should they release", says Superintendent Frank Hanlon, former garda press officer[34].

The garda spokesperson's hands are tied. She cannot release the name of a suspect, nor say where a search is taking place. Often she cannot comment, much as she would like to. Certain information has to be witheld for security reasons, because once released it is no longer security and the advantage can go to the criminal.

The strict sub judice rules in Ireland are very different from the US where the arresting officer can tell everything, freely mixing fact with speculation, regardless of how it might affect a later court hearing. One need only recall the Ben Dunne case in Florida when the supermarket chief was charged with a drug offence.

The Garda public relations department was established in 1972, following the report of the Conroy Commission[35]. It deals centrally with the media and reports directly to the office of the Commissioner, but much media relations has to be at local level and local officers have to be confident, articulate and accurate. All senior officers are now trained in media and presentation skills as well as other areas of management

The gardaí need public co-operation and the help of the media in detecting crime and for the success of public information campaigns, such as anti-drink/driving at Christmas.

They are an essential information source for the crime journalist and it is important that they avoid manipulation and deceit. The temptation is there to use the media for their own interests, rather than in the public good, with truth being the loser.

Former Scotland Yard commissioner, Sir Robert Mark, was aware that police media relations could easily become a propaganda weapon when he wrote that "police/public relations are not governed by the truth necessarily. They are governed by the appearance of the truth"[36]. He described the relationship between the police and the press as "an enduring, if not ecstatically happy marriage. We help each other in difficulties, tolerate each other's faults and try to promote each other's interests without too much disregard of our own"[37].

As commissioner, Mark initiated a very open policy with the media. He said:"It is my firm belief that the Metropolitan Police have a great deal more to be proud of than the public know and that a little more openness with the news media, heightening trust, confidence and co-operation, is all that is required to correct that ignorance"[38].

Community relations

The traditional garda on the beat was the ideal person to get to know the local people. One side of the work was to prevent and detect crime, but the other was to know the community and work for removing the sources and causes of crime. It is vital that young people grow up to see the gardai as social workers as well as law-enforcers.

This requires ongoing community relations programmes. It is too late for credibility to act only when local outrage builds up over an issue; community relations programmes must be in place in every community all of the time. The gardai must work with politicians, clergy, social workers, parents to build communities.

One problem in large cities is the difficulty for the gardai to know people as closely as in a small community. Cities mean that for the most part the gardai have to drive around in cars and motorbikes, making it harder to maintain the personal touch, witnessed in its extreme when they are stoned and beaten up by rampaging gangs.

41.   Government

"To us as communicators, the truth is the first commandment of our business and the pillar of our profession" - Larry Speakes, White House spokesman under President Ronald Reagan, 1981-87.[39]

IT MIGHT BE SAID that the whole work of Government is public relations. Every aspect of Government is concerned either with relationships, communication or reputation, but let three of the many issues be highlighted now - credibility, communication and damage limitation.

Credibility
        The Government must not only govern well, but must be seen to do so. Government must be credible and sincere and the cynicism of the ordinary voter has to be challenged.
        Governments have often given public relations a bad name - whether it be for projecting an image without any substance to back it up, or removing the facts from information and dispensing propaganda, or manipulating the news media. Public relations for government has, for some, been too professional, too slick. It used be handled by career civil servants who cleared their desks at 5 o'clock every evening. Now, an army of professionals, described variously as briefers, spin doctors, minders, handlers and fondlers are looking after the press round the clock.
        Topdog is the Government press secretary with her nods and winks and unattributable briefings. Nobody denies that her work is difficult. She must at once be "guru, buffer and interpreter on behalf of her boss - constantly reinterpreting the signals going in both directions"[40].
        It is amazing how easily the media acquiesce in this manipulation. They feel they cannot live without the Government press secretary who effectively fixes the agenda and decides what they should write and broadcast. In the Reagan years one journalist described his colleagues as "supporters with typewriters"[41].
        The Institute of Public Relations sponsored a debate at the

House of Commons, that "this House believes that effective public relations distorts the democratic process"[42]. Speakers were journalists, MPs and public relations people. One journalist attacked the "political public relations merchants who massage the media" and many references were made to Bernard "Sir Beelzebub" Ingham and his eleven years of work for Margaret Thatcher. In response, an MP claimed it was "ineffective" and not effective public relations which distorted the process and he cited the downfall of both Margaret Thatcher and Edwina Currie as examples. The 100-strong attendance passed the motion.

The apparent power and influence of the unelected Government press secretary often leads to resentment. Notable in Ireland, and not prepared to take any hostages, have been Peter Prendergast for the 1982-87 Fine Gael/Labour Coalition ("...a pressing force causing paranoia"[43]) and P.J.Mara for Fianna Fáil after 1987 ("a national fondler"[44]). Albert Reynolds appointed Seán Duignan, former RTE political correspondent, soft-spoken and one of the most popular journalists in Dublin, a contrast to the jovial but hard-hitting P.J.Mara who went on to be an adviser to the Guinness Peat Aviation Group.

Communication

Governments become enmeshed in the day-to-day problems of administration, legislation and troubleshooting, often forgetting to communicate what they are doing. They discover the cost of this lapse at election-time. Voters have short memories, strong prejudices and instinctive apathy.

Governments communicate their policies and achievements in many ways, but mostly through speeches in the Dáil, at annual conferences and at special functions. These are then reported in the media. But that is not enough because most people do not read those speeches and, if they do, they don't believe them.

Governments need to govern and to give strong leadership but in a democracy they also have to persuade. The social partners - employer and trade union organisations, and the many pressure groups, can not be bullied into submission. And they will not go away. They have to be persuaded to the government viewpoint. It is one thing to have a policy and a vision of what you want to do for the country; it is something else to win the support of those whose co-operation you need to make it all happen.

To persuade effectively, the Government has to ensure that those who go into bat for it are on top of their brief. They themselves have to be lobbyists.

There is now more professionalism in the use of radio and television interviews and photo opportunities, but still the risk of trivialisation through undignified gimmicks which are designed to grab attention but often lead to ridicule.

Politicians realise the importance of being properly prepared for television and radio. During their opposition years in the 1980s the complete Fianna Fáil front bench went to Carr Communications for courses in presentation and then made return visits hours before any serious interview. Some of them like to play this down now as they are accused of being lookalikes.

On election as Taoiseach, Albert Reynolds appointed Tom Savage, a director of Carr Communications, as communications adviser. This was a new post, in addition to Government press secretary and head of the Government Information Service. "I am in communications and analysis - not public relations", he told one interviewer[45]. (What, then, is public relations ?) He told another that his job was to devise structures which would make Reynolds' policy of open government a reality as well as dealing with the other "bits and pieces" of the communications role that were hanging over[46].

Damage limitation

It is dangerous to be in government. Disaster is always just round the corner and it hits when least expected. The crisis often comes not from policies which went wrong, or budget estimates which were inaccurate, but from one's friends and what they have done.

Some governments become accident-prone and this is often a prelude to electoral death. Remembering the GUBU Fianna Fáil government of 1982, many of their opponents saw comparisons in the business scandals in 1991[47].

Governments cannot ensure against all crises but they can

protect themselves by being prudent in their appointments and their choice of friends and by remembering that good public relations is not image-making, and that without substance, no amount of publicity stunts will be any use. The packaging of the Government has no credibility if performance does not live up to its promises and the slogans.

42. Local Government

"Meanness, distrust and abuse are the experience of the local govern-ment politician as he makes his essential contribution to the mainte-nance of local democracy in Ireland. Ministers of central government never tire of using local politicians as fall-guys for their own inepti-tudes, the press constantly denigrates and criticises but rarely devotes any time to an examination or an explanation of what's going on in local government" - Myles Tierney[48].

There are more than a hundred local authorities in Ireland. Operating under the Department of the Environment, they serve 1,500 elected councillors. Few of them pay any attention to public relations, but they are wrapped up in a succession of public relations issues. These include their own credibility, media coverage of their affairs and public suspicion about the way they behave.

Credibility

Myles Tierney writes that "politically, administratively and publicly, local government is the cinderella of our democracy"[49]. Central government has successively eroded powers from local authorities, so that finally some ask if have they a worthwhile role to play at all.

The strongest evidence of their power used to be the striking of the rate. Rates, although an inequitous tax, were an exercise in local democracy, money raised locally to be spent locally. When the government abolished domestic rates in 1977 local authorities no longer had that strong card to play, commercial rates attracting far less attention.

This power survives in some places, to a lesser extent, through service charges for water, refuse collection and the like. Councillors fight against them, even refusing to adopt the yearly budget which includes them. They defy the Minister who then threatens to dissolve them and replace them with a commissioner.

Councillors have to be lobbyists for themselves, and they start with the advantage of democratic platforms. Both inside and outside the chamber, they are local leaders, spokesmen on local issues and defenders of the people's rights and traditions.

Media coverage

Councillors complain that their meetings and decisions are not adequately covered in the media. That is certainly true in Dublin, where national papers find little that has a news relevance to a national readership. However, in the regions, the work of the local authorities is, with the courts, the principal source of news. Debates are reported on at length.

However, it is difficult for reporters to make news out of council meetings. One could sit for three hours listening to members drawing out tedious arguments and making ridiculous points of order, and get the complete news story worth publishing in about three minutes. The first-time reporter, indeed, is confused at the arcane procedures and does not know what is going on half of the time. To report properly she has to attend several times as well as mastering the principles of local government. She must be familiar with standing orders and with the ways and customs of the council and know the names, the faces, the voices, the opinions, the 'hobby horses' and background of the members.

Much that is reported originates outside the chamber as councillors take reporters aside and brief them. There is a lot of point-scoring between rivals and the reporter has to be wary. If councillors are to get better, and more constructive coverage of their activities, they should simplify their procedures. If they tackle serious issues, and speak seriously about them, they will get the coverage.

From time to time some let off steam with a bit of media

bashing. It gets them coverage in the local paper, and if it is funny enough, the nationals carry it, but it does nothing to convince the public that a serious job is being done and that more responsibility and power should be devolved from the centre. It can also backfire as an aside comment may be blown out of proportion or the councillor may be brought onto radio or television to explain it.

Councillors are bad at protecting their reputation. They are wary of public relations advisers, believing they can do the job themselves. They want to be first with the news, preferably a few minutes ahead of the members from the other party.

Dublin Corporation has had a public relations officer, Noel Carroll, since the early 1970s, but attempts to create a similar post in Dublin County Council failed, being resisted not only by the assistant county manager, Ruairí O Brolcháin, but by several councillors. One of them, Jim Guinan said: "We have 25 good public relations officers here and there is no need for another"[50].

The situation is different in Britain where local government is one of the busier areas of public relations. Typical advertisements in the press two years ago showed that Basildon Council, for instance, was seeking a new public relations officer. The post would cover press and media relations, conferences, marketing, exhibitions and the civic newspaper. "We're giving PR a higher priority at Basildon", the advertisement read. "We aim to involve local people in the running of their own community, so telling them about our policies and services is one of our most important tasks". Northamptonshire County Council was appointing a head of public relations "to spearhead a new high quality public relations function with a broad ranging brief to develop a PR strategy for the County Council. This will communicate our core values and build upon our image and profile with the community we serve, our customers and our staff". Brighton Borough Council wanted a press officer to "make waves at the seaside......by spreading the news about the Council's activities and all the services that we provide for the community"[51].

Trust

Councillors are not paid, but they get allowances for travel and for attending meetings. It will never make them rich but many see it as an apprenticeship for national politics, adding further to public cynicism. Suspicious and malicious people will always claim that, as there is no payment, people would not be there unless it provided some means of lining their own pockets. Allegations, not proved, have been made from time to time about councillors being bribed over land rezoning and planning permissions. The temptation is there, and councillors, in their behaviour and in the associates which they make in social and in business life, must be seen to be above reproach.

One media target is the councillors' 'foreign junkets'. When an authority, stretched for cash for essential services, sends a large contingent to an overseas conference, there has to be surprise. All of the parties defend it. They say that several councillors travelling is better than one. If only one went and reported an innovation in another country she might not be believed. But when six, from all parties, are visibly impressed, it is time for the others to think. In defence of foreign junkets, councillors claim new ideas and benefits which they have applied for better local government of their area. They point disparagingly at the junkets of ministers and of journalists.

43. Political parties

"Communications means throwing your net much wider than publicity. It means deciding what we say, how we say it, and which spokesmen and women we choose to say it" - Peter Mandelson, MP, former head of Communications and Campaigns for British Labour party[52].

PUBLIC RELATIONS for political parties creates awareness of the party and its policies, helps the leading figures to become better known, and provides information and research back-up, as well as supporting local officers in the constituencies. The past twenty years has seen a growing sophistication in the approach of the Irish parties, starting with Fianna Fáil when Séamus Brennan was general secretary and spreading to Fine Gael with Peter Prendergast.

Public relations, linked with party organisation at national and constituency level, has been recognised as a professional activity to be done by professionals. Key issues are internal communication, presentation of party policy, and 'dirty tricks'.

Internal communication

It is very easy for large parties to lose touch with their grassroots, unless there are clear policies for communication through all levels - front bench, parliamentary party, councillors, officers, ordinary members.

Backbench members of the parliamentary party should be briefed continuously, rather than finding out what their own party is doing only when a journalist asks them to comment. The grassroots must be kept in touch through visits by senior members, newsletters from head office and general maintenance of efficiency at branch level, so that meetings are properly held and delegates report back to their branches.

Constituency and branch officers need guidance and help with fund-raising and organising events. They need clear messages with sharp news angles which can gain coverage in the local media. When they knock on doors they must be seen to represent a party which knows what it is talking about, but this won't happen without strong leadership.

One sign that parties don't appreciate public relations at local level is that the most junior member in the branch is often given the job of public relations officer - impossible to do properly without experience and a thorough knowledge of the party and its history, policies and personalities.

Presentation of policy

Politics should be about policy and the serious issues facing the country, but it is inevitably dominated by personalities with strong opinions. Unity in the party is the ideal, rarely achieved, and when there are divisions it is better to be honest. But, when is a division really a division or merely some maverick trying to stir up the pot ?

Dáil and Seanad are the obvious but not the only platforms for presentation of party policy; the opportunities extend to meetings in every constituency, to county council chambers, factory openings and the like. Press, radio and television have an inexhaustible appetite for political comment. The local newspaper and radio station are an open door for any articulate local politician. This is an argument for a regional spread in the appointment of frontbench spokespeople.

Efficient presentation of party policy does not have to make it bland and toothless. It is impossible to please everybody all of the time and no party should try to do so. It is better to be honest and if one policy, for instance, favours the farmers, it is foolish to deny the countereffect it might have on PAYE workers in urban areas.

Members cannot comment from a vacuum. Headquarters must have an active research and information unit, analysing issues, articulating policy and writing guidelines for speeches. Never, however, should the same speech be supplied for seven different speakers in different parts of the country on one night, as Fine Gael did at one election.

Voters are used to professionals presenting the news and documentaries, and expect politicians to be as good in interviews and party political broadcasts. Standards have risen remarkably in recent years due to the grooming by the professionals, even if there is a certain stereotype in technique. But it is much better than what was there before.

Dirty tricks

Political parties are accused of dirty tricks - digging up scandal about their opponents, double voting, impersonating and so on. No party will admit to doing it and the leaders will claim not to know what their agents are doing. But it happens and no party can claim for itself a monopoly of virtue.

It is bad public relations because it is dishonest and it is usually found out. Public relations acts as the conscience of an organisation and it must push for the highest standards; otherwise it will be ineffective, carving rotten wood. The perception that many people believe all politicians to be crooks is not an excuse for them to live up to it.

One consultant decided once at election time that he would do his professional bit for his country. He went to Upper Mount Street in Dublin (where both Fianna Fáil and Fine Gael have their headquarters) and knocked on a door. He offered his services and was greeted. Put into a room, he was given the names of opposition candidates from all over the country. "Find out the dirt on each of them and get it to the right quarters", he was told.

Disgusted, he walked across the street to the other party. Again, a warm greeting, an invitation to sit down and work immediately. Again, a list of opposition candidates and, again, "find out the dirt". He went home.

Political parties have to struggle for credibility not just because of dirty tricks but because they are seen as propaganda machines. Few outside their own party believe them and nobody expects them to say anything good about their opponents. If they are to overcome this they have to build up respect. At the end of the day, as with all real public relations, they will be respected if they tell the truth.

Political parties are under growing pressure, especially from *The Sunday Tribune*, to make fuller disclosure about the sources of their funds. If a person or a business is a large contributor to party funds the public should be allowed to judge whether unfair favours have been given in return.

44.   Professional Bodies

"The concept of a business or professional association is a highly civilised one. It calls for what people do least well, subordinating their self interests to the betterment of all. And when members of the group are competitors, it seems an unnatural alliance that won't work. Yet it does, as the proliferation of associations has demonstrated" - Howard P. Hudson[53] .

PROFESSIONAL bodies normally restrict membership to suitably qualified practitioners of that profession. In the interests of the public good, some professions are registered by the Government and one cannot practice without being a member. Examples are medicine, dentistry, law, accountancy and nursing. Others are not registered, such as auctioneering, public relations, marketing and journalism.

It has been suggested that at least 75 % of the work of professional bodies falls within the field of public relations[54] . The work of the chief executive is essentially public relations. The priorities are to protect the reputation of the profession, communicate with members and lobby on their behalf.

Reputation

The professional body seeks to build and preserve the reputation of the profession and to show that it is deserved through special events and publicity for achievements of members, examination results, awards etc. It will publicise the professional and ethical standards which are required of members and respond to criticisms of the profession.

Often, a professional body only wakes up to public relations when it is under attack, but to be effective the public relations effort must be positive in its approach and its objective should be positively stated. "A programme devoted exclusively to answering attacks on a business is futile over the long term. After years of defensive efforts in public relations, an industry may find itself exactly where it began - or even in a poorer position"[55] .

The Marketing Institute of Ireland has in recent years boosted membership, enforced standards of education, expanded awareness of the profession and put on highly publicised events. It has achieved this partly through having a loose definition of what constitutes a marketing professional. To some extent, it acts on the basis that everybody in business is by that very fact, or should be, practicing marketing.

Some years ago a society was formed "for the protection of clients of the legal profession". It sought to expose rogue solicitors and get redress for clients who had been robbed or had received an otherwise poor service. This was some embarrassment to the Incorporated Law Society with the suggestion that it was not controlling its own members and was whitewashing complaints.

The Irish Auctioneers and Valuers Institute is the leading body representing its profession in Ireland and criteria for membership are strict. Its own survey of public attitudes towards the profession showed that more than 25 % of the population would not use one of them to sell a house and another 11 % were not sure. "This is a shocking reflection of the public's regard for the work and service of estate agents and auctioneers. Blame for it lies entirely within the profession itself", commented the Institute's journal[56].

Recognising the problems and saying all that it had done to improve the status of the profession - education, publications, compensation fund, nationwide advertising, brass nameplates, lobbying with the government, holding seminars, the journal added that the Institute could not change public opinion - "only members themselves can do this".

Public relations is not registered. Anybody is free to put up her name on her door and declare herself a public relations consultant and many still do without any qualifications or experience. The poor performance of some of these people further damages the reputation of public relations and adds to the popular confusion which surrounds it. However, it has been naive for public relations to put too much blame on the 'cowboys', while neglecting to look into its own heart.

Communication

Some professional bodies are sleepy outfits and it is very easy for them to lose touch with their members. They may be the only body for their profession and members feel they should belong, if for nothing else than to demonstrate that they are insiders and recognised by their peers.

Members usually expect services for their subscriptions, including regular communication and helpful professional information. This is done through newsletters, regular meetings of members, education and training, social events and platforms for speakers.

Presidents, elected for a fixed term, usually adopt a theme for their presidency and use every opportunity to publicise it. In the early

M

1980s the Public Relations Institute of Ireland emphasised education as it adopted qualifications and minimum entry requirements for new members, anticipating a similar move by the Institute of Public Relations in the UK which came into effect in 1992.

An active profession seeks new members. In public relations there are many professionals who have never been members of the Institute. The IPR in the UK has raised its membership from 2500 to 4000 within the past few years but this is still only an estimated 40 % of those who are practicing public relations in the UK.

Without a comprehensive membership it is difficult to enforce and maintain standards of professional practice and also difficult to be an effective lobbying voice.

Accountancy is a traditionally 'quiet' profession which has now discovered the importance of public relations. Until recently accountants were not allowed to publicise themselves. Now "public relations is absolutely crucial in our business", says one of the top British accountants. "We have about 200 target audiences for our various services, so advertising could not do the job effectively"[57] .

Lobbying

The professional body is a lobbyist for its members. The Confederation of Irish Industry, for example, embracing the whole of Irish industry, makes submissions on behalf of its members to Government committees, especially in advance of the budget. The CII is very much an insider body, listened to in government and civil service circles.

The Irish Hospital Consultants' Association was formed in the 1980s and it has quickly shown its muscle in negotiations with government, hospitals and the Voluntary Health Insurance Board.

On the other hand, there has been a tension between the Irish Farmers Association and successive governments. The farmers have suffered ever since their great national march on Dublin in 1966 when they came from all over the country to the Minister for Agriculture, Charles Haughey, and he left them camping out in the street refusing to meet them. It was a great march and they still talk about it, but in terms of achieving objectives it was like most students' marches, futile. In subsequent disputes there has remained a tendency for them to overreact and to adopt a threatening stance. The recent stunt when they herded a flock of sheep into the offices of the Department of Agriculture grabbed attention but gained little respect for them.

45. Public companies

"One cannot ignore the worldwide phenomenon of takeovers. However, in the case of Irish Distillers, the whole whiskey industry of Ireland which was built up over hundreds of years, fell to foreign ownership in one fell swoop. One can only ask what would the French or Italians or Spanish do if they saw their whole wine industries move to foreign ownership." - Professor Edward Cahill, University College, Cork[58].

PUBLIC COMPANIES, required to release all price-sensitive information first to the Stock Exchange, are different from private companies which, even with new EC directives, can still be very secretive about themselves.

An important issue for the quoted company is confidence. Also, being public, its problems are public, so that crisis management is important. Media relations have a special significance because of the influence which financial journalists have on investors and analysts.

Confidence

Confidence is reflected in the share price. On a bad day everybody's price is down, but if one is down more than others, or if it is down when the others are up, there is a major problem. There may be a reason such as bad results, or board or staff changes, or an EC or government decision which is affecting the sector adversely.

The investors are the audience whose confidence is most crucial. Unless they are kept fully informed they will not hold on to their shares, and a few selling suddenly becomes a panic. They will also be easy targets when a takeover bid is mounted.

The thrust of public relations is towards investors, with the annual report and other periodic statements requiring a lot of time and attention. The annual meeting can be a barometer of shareholders' feeling, but many of these meetings are poorly attended and carefully stage-managed by cunning chairmen. The result of this can be a cloud cuckoo-land which is soon disturbed by a predator buying up shares and leading a takeover bid.

Confidence among shareholders presupposes the confidence of the analysts who track a company and advise stockbrokers and investors when to buy and when to sell. They are not fooled by vacuous publicity. If there is a problem, it will not easily be concealed from them.

Crisis management

Private companies can have most of their crises in private, but not the public company. It will all come out. Anything which will cause the share price to drop is a crisis. The best way to prepare for a crisis is to prevent it. Preventable crises can result from mistakes in management and from failures to communicate or to act in time.

The frequent reaction to a crisis is to find a scapegoat upon whom all blame can be loaded. The hero one day can be villain the next. Examples have been Ernest Saunders with Guinness and Chris Comerford with Greencore, the former Irish Sugar Company.

The takeover bid is a crisis and unless the company has its strategy ready it will quickly lose the initiative in publicity and credibility to its attacker who has prepared for the moment and has all of her arguments ready. The negative response can be to run a slanging match with each side saying how unsuitable the other is to run the company. These negative campaigns are bad for both winners and losers because they lead to loss of confidence in the company.

In May 1988, the GC & C consortium, backed by the Grand Metropolitan Group, made a £200 million bid for Irish Distillers Group and it became the most highly publicised bid in Irish history with the board of Irish Distillers initially describing it as "ill-conceived, unsolicited and unwelcome"[59]. At the end Irish Distillers managed to beat it off, but the price was to accept a more friendly bidder, the French company Pernod Ricard. As a result, the Irish whiskey industry fell into foreign hands. Had the board of Irish Distillers, faced with the sale of the major Seagram shareholding and continuing poor performance in the export markets, responded earlier, say to Tony O'Reilly's soundings in 1987, the takeover might not have happened and the crisis might have been averted.

Media relations

Financial journalism was once nothing more than the listing of the stock exchange prices and ensuring no misprints occurred. Statements from companies were published without comment.

But that changed from the mid 1960s when *The Irish Times* set up a financial section and the weekly magazine *Business & Finance* was started. Soon, all of the papers had financial sections and the most recent sunday paper, *The Sunday Business Post*, was founded principally as a business and financial paper.

Nowadays, everything that happens in a public company is scrutinised by the journalists who are mostly highly-qualified and experienced and more knowledgeable on the subject than their sources or their readers. Financial columnists are read eagerly both by business executives and by investors. Their judgement is respected and their recommendations to buy or sell are acted upon.

Acres of newsprint to fill means an insatiable appetite for news and comment. Well managed public relations, with stories timed correctly and the right angles developed, can result in a lot of timely comment for a company, boosting shareprices in a completely legitimate manner. It is easier to get news into the financial pages than anywhere else in the paper. The lesson, of course, is that the wise public company should always employ professionals for its public relations.

46. Publishing

"There is an enormous amount of free editorial available to us in the press - a disproportionate amount, given how small the industry is compared to other consumer goods." - Martin Neild of Pan Macmillan[60].

MORE THAN 200 Irish book publishers release about 1,200 new titles a year. They face stiff competition with 60,000 new titles a year coming in from the UK. However, the Irish publishers have captured 30 % of the home book trade and a turnover of £70 million a year[61].

Public relations is important not just for publicity but also in dealing with authors and booksellers.

Authors

There was a time when authors could wallpaper their houses with rejection slips; nowadays 90 % of titles are commissioned by the publisher and the writer works closely with both her own agent and the publisher's editor.

Authors are a publisher's greatest asset. It is particularly hard for a small publisher to have discovered and nurtured a new writer, seen her through her early titles which made no money for anybody, and then to lose her to a larger competitor who pays her advances that cannot be matched.

Dealings with the author should go further than the legal contract. When publishers commission they often agree to pay royalties in advance, usually one part on commissioning, the next on delivery of final script and the final payment on publication. Then, no further payment until all of the advance has been recouped in sales. Publishers should be fair to their authors and pay proper advances. If they do not, somebody else will.

It is important to appreciate artistic integrity when editing an author's text. In books, as in newspapers, text has to be edited to eliminate careless writing, confusion and inaccuracy. But there is a difference between the book which may have been an author's total preoccupation for the several years and a news report written in half an hour. Greater sensitivity is required.

If the contract is to publish on an agreed date, then that should be done, or there must be a very good excuse and the author must be told in time. There should be no hedging on payments after publication.

Booksellers

Booksellers cannot plan properly for sales if the first warning about the book is its arrival on their doorstep. Publishers should stay in close contact during planning and production. Tell them what is happening and discuss in-store promotions and presentation. Publishers usually pay for the promotion and merchandising, although some say these costs should be shared with booksellers.

It might seem like the tail wagging the dog, but in the UK ten companies account for 70 % of book sales and in Ireland a chain like Easons, with its distribution as well as its retail arm, can make or break a new title. Publishers sending advance blurbs to booksellers sometimes get them back saying they are rubbish and the book won't be stocked or sold unless the cover is jazzed up.

New titles are sometimes planned in advance as major best-sellers and the entire promotional and public relations effort sets out to achieve that. Many hyped titles fail but the industry is resilient. "Gone to-day, here to-morrow" is the slogan, as lorryloads of a new gushy title go out one day, collapse like a pancake at the shops and come back a few weeks or months later to be pulped.

Gill and Macmillan had an exceptionally high promotional budget of £26,000 for the Gay Byrne autobiography, *The Time of My Life*, published in 1989. They did 60,000 hardback, which was the most ever for an Irish title and even high by UK standards. It came at the end of September to get the Christmas market. It was an immediate bestseller and a quick decision had to be made to reprint; the sales then died and many of the reprints were left on the shelves.

Publicity

Publicity does not start with publication but long before it. "The trick is to keep the momentum up during the book's gestation - that's where experience and track record count", says Louise Allen Jones, publicity manager of Bantam Press[62]. It could be said that unauthorised biographies of famous people are better in some ways than the authorised versions. If there is a constant flow of teasers, speculation as to what is in the book, what scandals will be uncovered, the news journalists will keep the pot boiling. In the UK, the mere hint of a kiss-and-tell book about a member of the royal family is enough for every gossip writer in the land to gush forth.

On publication, it is common practice to send out review copies to the media and to organise book signings. The book review pages are an important target for publicity, although the tastes of book editors are sometimes hard to comprehend and a certain snobbishness still affects some of them.

Launch parties are now held less frequently, and, even then, the publisher is less likely to offer free copies. One individualistic publisher, on producing an expensive book about the media, got the launch sponsored but chained sample copies to the tables. Those who wished to purchase could do so at the door. He did not send out any review copies.

Generally, the media are helpful. They welcome a book which can make a good news story, a feature article or a photo-opportunity. Nearly every book has angles which continue beyond the teasing stages of pre-publication. Not all authors achieve, nor would they like to achieve, the fame of Salman Rushdie with his *Satanic Verses*. It sparked a worldwide Muslim outrage leading to the Ayatollah Khomeini passing a death sentence on him which was not lifted even with the Ayatollah's death. Rushdie went into hiding, probably for ever, but the sales rocketed. By early 1991 they had reached one million in hardback and then the paperback edition was published. This was staggering as a hardback bestseller published in the UK is normally lucky to sell around 20,000 copies.

Getting the author onto radio and television shows is a help, but it is important to target the ideal programme. In RTE it is unlikely that the same author would be used by both the Pat Kenny and the Gay Byrne shows. Beyond these popular shows, however, there are those for specialist listeners and viewers. If the book is about angling and the author is interviewed on a radio programme for anglers there is immediate contact with virtually every potential buyer of the book.

Popular authors undertake worldwide promotional tours.

However, some are useless and have to be kept away from such tours and from signing sessions in shops. Before arranging a signing session, look at the type of people who read this author's books and judge honestly whether they would come out. One popular UK thriller writer flopped when he visited Ireland, yet his sales number millions. Other writers who are famous for some controversy have massive success, like John Stalker who was removed from the investigation into police behaviour in Northern Ireland. He appeared on the *Late Late Show* and next day there were queues half-way around Dublin when he came to sign his new book.

47. Retailing

"All aspects of public relations apply to retail stores, but retailing public relations has one major aim. That is to give the store visibility and identity. The store that loses out is the one that is lost in the crowd. Retailers who are regarded as 'outstanding citizens' are the ones whose stores never stop making a mark on the community, the employees, the manufacturers, and on the national scene as well" - *Terry Mayer*[63] .

SUPERMARKETS and department stores spend large sums achieving visibility and identity. The big ones and the people who run them, are household names. Their public relations includes marketing support, but it must not overlook the effect upon reputation of customer, staff and community relations as well as crisis planning.

Marketing support
   In general, retailers spend on formal public relations about one tenth of what they spend on advertising and promotions. Their public relations includes media attention for opening of new stores, special promotions, bargain offers and the like. But it is also an advisory and planning function, standing outside and viewing the operation objectively. It is a means for the market to answer back.

Public relations advice is required before changes are made or new ventures undertaken to be aware of their community impact and effect upon reputation. The community's attitude towards the store must be analysed constantly.

Care is needed, for instance, not to exploit children through promotional events, an anxiety which arose initially with a Quinnsworth offer, whereby schools got computers in return for the amount of checkout receipts which the children collected. There was fear of undue pressure on less well-off parents, but it was then specified that they did not have to be one's own purchases. So, enterprising children took up position at checkouts to collect shoppers' receipts.

Also, some retailers jumped upon the green bandwagon merely as a marketing gimmick and ignored its public relations potential. They missed out on the chance to inform and educate their customers and, as a result, very few people have been convinced or impressed by some of their claims.

Retailers often see media relations as getting plugs for non-newsworthy events, what they themselves would call 'free publicity'. Or they see it as the way to show their strength, threatening withdrawal of their massive advertising budget if they get critical treatment. That bluff is easily called because they would not be spending that money in the first instance if they were not already convinced that they needed the advertising; so why cut off their bottom line to spite their thin skin.

Customer relations

It is easy to forget the primacy of the customer in the midst of detailed management of the business. "Good customer relations are the essence of the success of Marks and Spencer. Even Arabs visit their stores ! It was the basis of Jesse Boot's success when he laid out his medicines on an open counter where people could see them. It was Gordon Selfridge who made shopping fun. There is nothing new about developing good customer relations"[64].

Feargal Quinn's boomerang principle must be remembered; treat every customer as a potential repeat customer and you will be all right. Even Dunnes Stores, for long dismissive of public relations, are now realising that there is more to success than slogans like

"Dunnes Stores better value beats them all".

Anita Roddick sees customer care as the "number one priority in the retail trade. If you make your product good and you make your store a pleasant place to be in, people won't object to paying your prices"[65].

Staff and community relations are closely bound up with customer relations. The supermarket is often judged by the attitude of the person at the checkout. Customers are reluctant to shop in a supermarket when they hear on radio that female staff have been sacked for going to the toilet (that has happened !).

Customers are also critical of poor community relations. A serious issue in Dublin is the illegal street traders. There is certain sympathy for them because of their long tradition in the city of Molly Malone who "wheeled her wheelbarrow through streets broad and narrow, crying cockles and mussels, alive, alive oh" but the large and small businesses (and the licensed street traders) who pay rents and rates are being unfairly hit. Overreaction can lead to unfavourable publicity as has happened a few times with the Dublin City Centre Business Association.

Crisis planning

Retailers are vulnerable to major crises: problems in the conglomerates which own them (Switzer's and the House of Fraser), kidnap of the chief executive (Dunnes Stores and Quinnsworth), or fire (twice to Superquinn within a few months), or terrorist attack (frequently with incendiary devices), or contamination of product, or staff dispute (Clery's had a crippling 14-week dispute in 1983; Dunnes Stores gained worldwide publicity when staff were dismissed for refusing to handle South African fruit).

These crises cannot always be prevented but good public relations means planning for them. Part of the preparation is to build up of credibility with the media. When Ben Dunne, chief of Dunnes Stores, was kidnapped by the IRA, his longstanding reticence towards the press acted against the company. It was not used to dealing with the media and was unable to kill the unfavourable publicity over, for instance, whether or not a ransom had been paid. However, Dunne learnt the lesson and when he was arrested for a drugs offence in the US in 1992 he gave the full details and apologised, leaving no room for further rumour. He was respected for his courage and, most importantly, damage to the company was limited.

When Superquinn's head office and supermarket in Sutton were destroyed by fire, they implemented crisis plans instantly ensuring accurate communication with the media, information and assistance for customers, proper treatment of staff and the quick resumption of full services. For instance, they provided pickup points to collect customers' orders and to deliver to them from other stores in the group. Also, they offered free travel for Sutton shoppers to other stores. Within a day of the fire, the head office staff had been relocated in the new centre which at the time was being built in Blackrock and the architects' plans were being drawn up to rebuild on the Sutton site.

48. Roman Catholic Church

"I have been critical and remain critical of how the media treat the Catholic Church in Ireland.........more than two-thirds of those surveyed in 1984 were of the opinion that the Catholic Church is often wrongly criticised in the media" - Bishop Brendan Comiskey of Ferns[66].

THE ROMAN Catholic Church was quick to realise the value of modern communications and public relations. It addressed the issue in a Vatican Council document of 1963 which though "the slightest document"[67] of that Council, was at least an official recognition of the media of social communication.

Before RTE was set up, Archbishop John Charles McQuaid of Dublin had allowed two of his priests, Joe Dunn and Desmond Forristal, to visit the USA to study television techniques. One result was the *Radharc* television documentaries which are still explaining the work of the church and the issues which must concern it at home and abroad.

The Dublin Diocesan Press Office, headed by a journalist, Osmond Dowling, was set up soon after the Vatican document. Later, the bishops established the Communications Centre in Booterstown to train clergy in television presentation, and also modernised their publishing and bookselling activities.

There are many public relations issues facing the Catholic Church in Ireland, but three of the most relevant are preservation and presentation of doctrine, handling of crises and conflicts and the use of lobbying.

Preservation and presentation

The Christian message is 2,000 years old and unchanging. But in all ages this message has needed translation so that people of the day can understand it and apply it to their lives.

Church communication involves propaganda. It is presenting matters of faith which cannot be proven; otherwise, it would not require faith to believe them ! Its message is essentially one-sided, because in talking of virtue, it cannot concede any good arguments to the devil. It can show that it is reasonable to believe, but has to assume the truth in the belief.

Traditionally, the church has communicated through preaching and writing. The Gospels were an early example of excellent communications. So has been the worldwide missionary movement. A complex message was told simply and in language that all could feel they understood. Nowadays the church uses the mass media to get quicker to a greater audience, but it is a more critical audience, and the message has to compete with many others.

The Catholic Church is expert in arranging the big public event. The Pope's visit to Ireland in 1979 was spectacular, with more than 3,000 journalists accredited and almost every member of the Public Relations Institute of Ireland helping in some way.

Irish newspapers used publish in detail the Lenten pastoral letters of the bishops. That is not possible now but there is still very full treatment of religion. All serious statements, documents and meetings are reported and commented upon. Since the mid 1960s each national paper has had a religious correspondent.

Some members of the clergy, however, have formed an obsession about the media. They tend to exaggerate its influence and, overlooking the power of other channels of communication, they feel that the media should be a propaganda arm for them because most of the journalists profess to be Catholic.

They feel that people in the media are out to get them. Such papers as *The Irish Catholic*   regularly give out about the 'secular press' and Fr. Martin Tierney, director of the Catholic Communications Institute of Ireland has said that "the only people who don't appreciate how despised they are are the journalists themselves"[68].

Bishop Joseph Duffy of Clogher told *The Sunday Tribune* that "if the media does not reflect the underlying Christian values of our society, then the Church will continue to decline and the quality of life will continue to suffer"[69]. One student commented that the bishop overlooked the "adequate media coverage and alternative publicity not only from the pulpit every weekend, but also through their own magazines and journals". She added that "Bishop Duffy seems to say that the Catholic Church and christian values are almost extinct if not covered by the media". In her view his statement would be absolutely correct if one substituted the word "church" for "media"[70].

Handling of conflicts

The church cannot always choose the agenda for debate; the media select what will interest their readers. The Pope is praised, but also criticised. There is concern at 100,000 priests leaving their ministry in the past 20 years, and at priests not being allowed to marry, nor women to become priests at all. The method of appointing bishops, and the sort of people whom the Pope promotes, provokes heated debate. The Catholic Church is accused of being obsessed with sex. People wonder why the Church of Christ could accumulate such material wealth and then lose so much of it through financial scandals.

The official response to crisis is usually inadequate and often a matter of keeping quiet and hoping it will all blow over. The official church should come up front and pre-empt its critics. If there is bad news, let it be the first to declare it and get in its case before the attack.

There is clearly a great embarrassment that the ordinary faithful will be scandalised by disclosure. When Archbishop McQuaid of Dublin returned from the Vatican Council in December 1965, he told a gathering in Dublin's Pro-Cathedral: "You may have been worried about much talk of changes to come. Allow me to reassure you. No change will worry the tranquillity of your Christian lives"[71].

It has been a new experience for the Catholic Church to have to react publicly to crisis and conflict within its own ranks. One might have thought they could learn by experience, but the resignation of Bishop Eamonn Casey of Galway has shown otherwise. It is unprecedented for an Irish bishop, indeed almost for any modern bishop, to have to admit that he has a 17-year-old son and that he has borrowed church funds to support him and his mother. Instead of coming up front, like Ben Dunne, making a complete statement and apologising, the bishop issued an innocuous and incomplete statement through the Catholic Press Office. As a result, rumour took over and story was front page for a week instead of two days. If he had given a press conference, told the whole story himself, and allowed no margin for rumour, he could have resigned with some dignity. Instead, he ran away to America as if he were a fugitive from justice.

Power of lobbying

The Catholic Church in Ireland is a legitimate and powerful pressure group. Its message has impact when it really wants to make itself heard. It does not falter in its campaign, but realises the power of repetition and selects the angle of the argument most suited to its audience at any particular time.

In lobbying, it surpasses all other groups. On the one hand it deals behind the scenes with those who can influence decision-making. Up front, it can co-ordinate the preaching from its pulpits. It then has the skill to use every medium of communication to keep the message alive. In Ireland, it has chosen its platforms carefully. Clashes between Church and State have been few. The two most recent instances, where the Catholic Church pulled out all the stops and used its communications and public relations skills to the extreme, and successfully, were the abortion and divorce referenda in the mid 1980s.

Those who lost those battles should not quibble. They were beaten by a better team on the day; a team that used all of its resources and was far more skilled and sophisticated in its public relations. Any other pressure group, with similarly strong cards to play, would, or at least should have, done the same. It is nonsense to say the church should keep out of politics. It never has, and it does not to-day, whether it be in South America, The Philippines, Poland or Ireland.

49. State bodies

"It is probable that when any semi-state board becomes the centre of controversy - as is not unlikely at some period of its existence - its independence is likely to be in serious jeopardy, because Ministers, realising the folly of accepting responsibility without effective power, will be disposed to bring their operations under closer supervision, which could reduce if not eliminate their special utility as an administrative device." - Sean Lemass[72].

THERE ARE about a hundred state bodies (also referred to as semi-state or state-sponsored). The original idea was to provide important commercial and social services which the private sector was unsuitable, unwilling or unable to provide. Some of these bodies, like Aer Lingus, are commercial. Others, like Bord Failte, are promotional. Others, like Coras Iompar Eireann, are commercial but also expected to provide a social service. To do their jobs properly they need some of the freedoms of industry without the restraints of civil service procedure. Each has a minister under whose aegis it operates, and to whom it has to answer.

The first state bodies - ESB, Agricultural Credit Corporation and the Sugar Company were set up in the 1920s. Now, there is a move towards privatisation with others likely to follow the Sugar Company and Irish Life.

Generally, the state bodies have been conscious of public relations, the ESB in 1927 being the first public utility organisation in Europe to appoint a public relations officer.

The main public relations issues facing state bodies at present are demonstrating that they operate efficiently and honestly and give value for money, recruiting and keeping top personnel and preparing for privatisation.

Value for money
The taxpayer, paying totally or partially for these bodies, is annoyed at any appearance of inefficiency, waste or scandal. The financial controversies of 1991 had added significance because they concerned Greencore, the privatised former Sugar Company and the matters raised occurred when it was a state company, and Telecom Eireann which seemed to pay over the odds for its new headquarters in Ballsbridge. State bodies do not like controversy; therefore one feature of their public relations function should be anticipation and, where possible, prevention of controversy. As Lemass said, Ministers do not like to be embarrassed and they will find ways to clip the wings of any body which is unduly controversial.

The promotional and service bodies have to demonstrate that they are doing a job - Bord Failte, that the tourists would not have come otherwise, and the IDA, that its efforts are cost-effective and create new jobs. These bodies lack a competitor to measure themselves against and their statements are therefore easily dismissed as propaganda.

All of them are involved extensively in public relations work, publications, speech-making and promotional activities. They are obliged to produce annual reports, but the presentation of these reports can lead to criticism that they are wasting money on the ego massage of their executives and engaging in a cosmetic exercise.

The commercial bodies have to be as good as their competitors. Some, like Aer Lingus and Radio Telefis Eireann have had to compete with bigger, better-financed outside organisations like British Airways and the BBC. It is only in recent years that there was been home competition for Aer Lingus in Ryanair and for RTE in the independent radio stations.

Recruitment of top personnel
The Devlin report of 1972 drew up different pay scales for chief executives based on the size of their organisations[73]. In all cases the

N

rates were less than executives with similar responsibilities would earn in the private sector. The pay ceilings for chief executives filter down through the organisation, with frustration and the loss of many good people to the private sector. The Greencore controversy arose partly because of efforts to give extra emoluments to executives.

Ireland was lucky that the pioneering people who saw the major bodies through their early, hungry years put public service before personal gain. Examples among many would be Tim O'Driscoll of Bord Failte, Jerry Dempsey of Aer Lingus, General Michael Joe Costello of the Sugar Company and Tom Walsh of the Agricultural Institute. They could have earned fortunes in the private sector.

To get and keep the best people, the state sector must be ready to lobby government for more realistic pay scales, and that will succeed only if they have already shown that they are giving value for money.

They also need employee communication programmes, so that staff will take pride in the organisation and want to work for it. Staff need to know what the organisation is and where it is going and how they are part of its plans. They can get worried about their future, because the old experience of a safe, pensionable job for life no longer holds, as seen in the closure of Irish Shipping and the sale of B & I Shipping to the private sector.

Preparation for privatisation

The Irish Government shares the privatisation philosophy of the British Government and wants to pass to the private sector some of the responsibilities which nowadays it can do more profitably.

The public relations used in the preparation of any private company for the stock market apply also to privatisations of state bodies. These involve making the company and its value known to and appreciated by potential corporate and private investors, and building up confidence in it. But with state bodies, there is also a desire to involve as many small shareholders as possible.

Trade unions might not like privatisation, but with present government thinking they are unlikely to have much choice about it. It is the same as in private industry. If a major shareholder in a large company like Smurfit or Guinness decides to sell her stake, it is not seen as a matter for the unions, even if they show concern.

50.   Tourism

"It was at the opening of the festival that Mulligan made his famous 'Small is Wonderful' speech, catching the ear of Gerald Craig, recently appointed chief executive of the Board of Welcomes. Craig had been searching for someone with the grit and gumption and personality to convince an apathetic populace that they had the wherewithal to make Ireland what Craig called 'the playground of Europe" - David Hanly[74].

TOURISM supports 73,500 jobs in Ireland. Foreign currency earnings from tourism were £1,139 million in 1990 and the Government grant for Bord Fáilte Eireann - The Irish Tourist Board, was £22 million for 1991.

The promotion and development of tourism involves much attention to public relations. Priority issues are news from Ireland, awareness and promotion of tourism products, and the support of influential audiences.

News from Ireland
Tourist boards everywhere bring in foreign journalists, wining and dining them and showing what the country can offer. When they go home they write copiously, and usually favourably, about their experiences. This will change as newspapers strengthen their ethical codes and become less willing to accept such support.

Many come at their own expense and are assisted by Bord Fáilte in getting to the right places and people, as instanced hilariously and bawdily in David Hanly's novel, *In Guilt and in Glory*. Hanly, now an RTE broadcaster, was publicity officer for Bord Fáilte in the 1970s.

Public relations cannot eliminate publicity which is harmful to tourism, but crisis plans must be ready for when such publicity happens.

For more than twenty years the Northern troubles have been providing bad news about Ireland. Bord Fáilte has had to neutralise its distortions and show that the Republic is not at war and is a safe place to visit. But every fresh atrocity starts the problem all over again.

Some also feel that reports of tourists being mugged and robbed in Dublin, films like *The Commitments* showing the deprived areas of North Dublin, and news features about the treatment of the travelling people do not help. However, real public relations does not sanitise the truth, but accepts that Ireland has the same problems as any other country.

Promotion of tourism products

Ireland cannot be sold to tourists on the basis of sun, sand and sea because it rains too often. Tourists don't come to Ireland just for the weather, they can be attracted by an extensive and lively array of tourism products - sports, festivals, exhibitions, medieval banquets, folk parks, special events, and just the scenery and the quiet of the countryside.

Local initiative is important, as with Dr. T.J.Walsh who created the Wexford Opera Festival in the 1950s, now stronger than ever and a valuable earner of tourism revenue. The Rose of Tralee Festival has been running for more than 30 years and is supported worldwide. The Tidy Towns Contest promotes initiative everywhere, an outstanding success which has done much for local pride and beautified the whole countryside.

Ireland is also promoted as a conference centre, giving year-round tourism. It is ideally located between America and the rest of Europe, with beautiful locations and top class facilities in every region. The last European Presidency was used deliberately to show the facilities out of Dublin such as Ashford Castle in Cong and Dromoland Castle in Clare.

The Convention Bureau of Ireland is the promotional arm of Bord Fáilte which brings together the main organisations that provide services to conferences, business meetings and incentive travel. In 1990, this business brought 89,000 people to Ireland.

Bord Fáilte and the six regional tourism organisations, whose activities it co-ordinates, provide support for the organisers of all these special holiday and tourist events. While there were three million foreign visitors to Ireland in 1990, there was also an income of £342 million from home holidays.

Tourism is a very sensitive business - everybody has at least one horror travel story to tell. Public relations for tourism is to some extent selling dreams, but the reality very often fails to match. With most people it is their major expenditure in the year, the outcome of much longing and dreaming. One must ensure not to over-promise. As with Feargal Quinn and his boomerang principle - you may get a tourist once, but if you don't satisfy, you will never get her back again. Nor will you get her family and friends.

Winning support

Bord Failte depends on its Government grant. It is therefore essential for government and for all who can influence government to be convinced of the importance of tourism and of Bord Failte's role. It can be easily forgotten behind the higher profile of new industry and the millions of pounds spent attracting overseas firms.

One tactic is the creation of opportunities for speakers. The Minister attends tourism events all over the country and makes speeches at them, as do the senior executives of Bord Failte and of the other tourist organisations. The presence of these people and their encouraging words are a support to local initiative and gain local and national media coverage. Speechwriting is an important tool in Bord Failte's public relations, stressing the achievements and social and economic benefits of tourism.

In addition to the travel brochures published by the commercial companies, the tourist bodies have an extensive programme of publications, ranging from the Bord Failte annual report to other corporate publications, results of research surveys, information leaflets on specific tourist activities and guidebooks for everything that the tourist might possibly want to know. These have to be glossy and expensive because they are competing with high quality products from abroad.

51.   Trade Unions

"With regard to trade union activity, the media tend to judge the overwhelming bulk of it - in the fields of salary negotiation, grievance procedures, productivity agreements, health protection - to be without significance, while the relatively small amount of energy devoted to withdrawal of labour is supposedly central" - Daltún O Ceallaigh[75].

TRADITIONALLY, trade unions have been bad at public relations. They are geared to confrontation and most of their communication takes place during disputes or threats of disputes. But, they need to look after themselves in times of peace as well as war, and in their public relations they must look first to their key audiences, who are management, their members and the general public.

Management
    Trade union officials do not make easy bed-fellows with management, for they do not want to be seen by their members to lose face. However, recent years have seen a greater maturity and effective lobbying by the Irish Congress of Trade Unions (ICTU), in partnership with employers and Government, has brought considerable industrial peace.
    The message that unions give to management is not always the correct one, and management realise that the ordinary worker does not always hold the same view as her union leader. The easiest strategy then is to divide and conquer; appeal to the ordinary member over the head of the union leaders, as Michael Edwardes did very effectively during the British Leyland disputes of the late 1970s.
    For unions to be credible to management, they must show that they represent all of their members. They should go to the ordinary member and not let management take the initiative away from them. This might mean changing their line because the ordinary member will rarely feel as strongly as the militants on any issue. However, the role of the union should be not just to make the strongest case possible to management, but to make the case that most accurately reflects what its members want.

Members

Unions need to communicate regularly with their members to build up an understanding which can be a reservoir of good will when fire breaks out. The ICTU is particularly diligent in this regard, through a comprehensive range of publications, meetings, courses and seminars. European and women's issues and the rights of part-time workers feature in recent activity. Its information office compiles research and provides general information to member unions.

In 1990/91, unions organised 91 courses with the assistance of ICTU. There were also courses for special groups - women representatives, safety representatives, worker directors, officials and tutors - as well as a three-day course in media relations[76].

Many members don't attend union meetings, but allow decisions to be taken by small groups of activists, see their union only as a fire brigade, forgotten about in good times but available immediately when a problem occurs. Unions cannot be effective if this is the practice.

The general public

ICTU has a "positive profile programme" as part of its strategy to promote trade unionism. It receives a growing number of invitations to address vocational, religious, community, educational, cultural and media organisations. "These invitations provide important opportunities for presenting a trade union perspective on current issues to groups who often know very little about trade union policies"[77]. It is also involved in other promotional activities like display stands, advertisements, sponsorships and festivals.

It is difficult to maintain a "positive profile" when so much publicity for trade unions centres around disputes. And, how much communication is advisable during a dispute ? At that stage some would argue that it is too late to convince the general public. They have lost their electricity, their buses, their post and whatnot - the damage has been done.

Throughout the British coal-miners strike of 1984/5, the National Union of Miners had one press officer at its head office, doubling as personal assistant to the president, Arthur Scargill, who was already a hate figure with the tabloid press. She had to contend with more than 100 journalists covering the story each day. The National Coal Board had over 40 press officers efficiently co-ordinated throughout the country, with their press releases and briefings carefully planned and timed to their best advantage. By all accounts they won the information war, but it was a bloody victory and in its wake both management and unions in Britain have adopted a low key approach to the press.

Some now feel that it is unwise to provide a lot of information during a dispute. If the profile it too high positions can become more entrenched with both sides afraid to compromise through fear of seeming to let their members down, and the strike is prolonged.

Unions often act before trying to tell the general public what the issue is; they defy all of the rules of good lobbying by dramatising their case before they have demonstrated to a wider public than themselves that there is an inequality that must be put right.

The ordinary person who suddenly finds her electricity cut off, her buses idle, her letters undelivered, her bins not emptied, is too angry to start wondering if the strikers have a case. But if she is already convinced that there is an injustice and that every other means has been tried unsuccessfully with a stubborn management, then she might be more willing to put up with the inconvenience.

Says Daltún O Ceallaigh: "Trade unionists are usually either hostile or indifferent to the media. Hostility is a reaction to the bad image which, they feel, the media give them in the form of sensationalist and unbalanced coverage. Indifference, on the other hand, springs from the belief that what press, radio and television say does not really matter much to industrial affairs at the end of all, and more fatalistically perhaps, from the conviction that it is virtually impossible to get a fairer crack of the whip anyway"[78].

O Ceallaigh, formerly information officer for ITGWU, is now general secretary of the Irish Federation of University Teachers. He points out that there is practically no end to the ways in which selected facts can be treated so as to convey one meaning to the exclusion of another. "Vocabulary, atmosphere, story angles, detail given, and of course, judicious use of photographs can all add up to the construction of a message which many trade unionists would regard as at variance with reality"[79].

He instances loaded words in reports of industrial disputes, with decentralised collective bargaining becoming a 'free for all', militancy being mindless' and socialism, but never capitalism, being 'doctrinaire'. Pickets gathering in numbers are said to be 'mobbing' and if pushed back by the Gardai they are 'battling' with the police.

Research during the Reagan era in the US showed that "on television, in general, unions were almost invisible. Whenever they did appear, in general, the massive tendency in popular culture was that unions were depicted as violent, degrading and obstructionist. When unionised occupations were looked at...... workers were depicted as clumsy, uneducated fools who drink and smoke too much and have no leadership ability"[80].

52. Universities

"The University of Limerick is dedicated to the pursuit of excellence in teaching and research: it combines this dedication with a concern for relevance to the needs of the students and the community" - Dr. *Edward Walsh, President, University of Limerick, 1991*[81].

UNIVERSITIES cannot lock themselves in ivory towers, dispensing learning purely for its own sake. They have to compete in the marketplace for the best staff and students; to be concerned with how they present themselves not just to staff and students but also to their external audiences.

Three central issues in public relations for a university today are relevance, excellence and funding.

Relevance

Students are concerned about what they will be able to do at the end of their courses and the jobs for which they will be suited. It is not enough to be learned but the learning has to be relevant to jobs with curricula flexible to meet the changing needs of students, industry and society. This relevance has to be reflected in the university's achievements and how it publicises them.

Relevance is aided through faculty members being involved in their professions, through research and employment linkages with industry, and through students gaining work experience and enriching the campus. The University of Limerick and Dublin City University have been very alert to this need and, having grown from green fields over the past twenty years, they have had flexibility built into them. It is interesting, however, that Trinity College has been the first Irish university to join the Confederation of Irish Industry.

Some question this new concept of relevance. A lecturer at the University of Limerick, Patricia Palmer, feeling that the arts have little place in her president's notion of relevance, has responded: "What is relevant to UL is that which is relevant to the operation of the free market. It will supply the market with the skills and, almost more importantly, the attitudes it needs. The critical imagination that might challenge this definition of the 'relevant' is far from being 'irrelevant': its analytical impulse rather is all too pertinent - and therefore excluded"[82].

Professor Joe Lee, from University College Cork, raises the same question, criticising the official mind which "embraced the ideology of high technology with little grasp of the criteria by which it might assess and control the performance of this new wonder drug". He asks to what do the technologists want education to be 'relevant'. "To a strategy of national development ? That issue was delicately avoided. The technologists, as technologists, had themselves no qualifications for assessing national or social 'relevance"[83].

Excellence

The university has to be excellent in its teaching and its research but also in the environment which it creates. The campus must reflect the needs of the complete person, providing learning for life as well as for work.

One strategy to enhance excellence is to develop academic and research linkages with other, renowned institutions so that some of their excellence can rub off. A reputation for excellence can also be helped through hosting of international conferences, appointment of visiting professors, endowed chairs and even sponsored schools, as in the Michael Smurfit School of Business at University College, Dublin.

The university of today has to talk not just to its faculty and students, but to a broader educational world, industry, the professions, financial institutions, politicians, the taxpaying public. The excellent university is quick to tell how its students have obtained employment in the best companies, how they have developed as entrepreneurs, how they have obtained prestigious research grants, how they have contributed to the community.

University status has long been seen as a symbol of excellence, and the traditional universities jealously guard it. Other institutions have conducted vigorous lobbies to gain it, but the new universities at Limerick and north Dublin are only the first since the foundation of the state in 1922.

It has been different in the UK where the Government has recently designated 35 polytechnics as universities giving them great excitement as they re-name themselves. For instance, Leicester Polytechnic, in becoming De Montfort University, proclaimed that "behind the name is a well-established institution with an outstanding record in research and consultancy and a formidable international reputation"[84]. A spokesperson for the new university said: "We wanted a name that wasn't nondescript. Polytechnics have always had a problem projecting themselves abroad and market research tells us that overseas students like the idea of it"[85].

The older universities are worried, with one professor from Oxford University saying that "the re-naming of polytechnics as universities will change the nature of what it is to be a graduate and lead to a diminishing respect for the British university degree around the world"[86].

Funding

Universities must compete to survive. And, to compete, they can no longer be content with handouts from government, they must find other ways to fund themselves. This means new forms of sponsorship and partnership with industry for academic and research programmes and expansion of buildings and student facilities,

Celebrating its 400th birthday in 1992, The University of Dublin (Trinity College) had a lot to be proud of and to boast about, and it did not spare any effort in making the most of the occasion to enhance its reputation for relevance and excellence and to help its fundraising. It now has almost 10,000 students and is the first choice of more degree students than any other university in Ireland, a big change from the 1950s when the Roman Catholic Church banned its members from attending.

Alumni associations are another source for funds, intended not just to help past graduates to network, but to provide a pool which can give something back. The Royal College of Surgeons in Ireland, not funded by the State, has to rely heavily upon its graduates, many of whom are wealthy foreigners living abroad.

The danger in a scramble for funding is a dilution in excellence. It has happened to some of the British universities, competing with each other at educational fairs in places like Hong Kong. There, the academics perform like travelling salesmen offering special offers and cuts in qualification standards to get overseas students and their money for the cash-starved university at home. Also, dilution can occur through an over-enthusiastic approach to franchising, that is licencing institutions abroad to prepare students on their own for an award to be granted by the home university.

53.   War

"The first casualty when war comes is truth" - *Senator Hiram Johnson, 1917.*

OUR LEADERS have never told us the truth in time of war and it is unlikely that they ever will. Public relations is extremely relevant in war, and, unfortunately, superbly effective.

All of the preceding chapters have emphasised the importance of truth in public relations, and to an outside reader, may be over-pleading a special case on behalf of the public relations profession. But, without any excuse, truth has to be the prime duty in public relations, if society is to remain civilised.

War, and the jingoism and triumphalism that go with it, are a shame to governments and to the people whom they represent. War is a shame to those journalists who go with the system, but happily there are journalists who do not submit and who try to tell the world what is really happening. War is a shame to the public relations profession, for the truth is rarely told, and whatever truth there is, is manipulated for unworthy purposes.

Arguments are made that some higher cause than the truth is being served, that if the truth were told the people would be demoralised, and the troops would die in even greater numbers, and it would take longer to overcome the enemy. But truth cannot allow exceptions; there is only one truth.

After each war, the generals and the politicians strike their breasts and say how sorry they are that the information systems were faulty and that journalists were not able to do their jobs properly, but they do not mean a word of it. It was said that generals spend each war planning how to win the previous one, but it is now true that the public relations, or more accurately, the propaganda machines, spend the intervals between war making sure that the next time none of the truth will get out.

Hiram Johnson made his oft-quoted remark about truth being the first casualty at a time when the USA had just entered World War I. That was the war after which the ordinary man in the trenches, fighting for the survival of small nations, while his generals wined and dined at a safe distance, realised for the first time that his newspapers told him lies. He was in his trench, thousands were dying around him, and yet his newspapers, sent to him from home, told of massive victories with minimal losses. He knew that the reporters, not let anywhere near the front, were telling the lies that the generals and their public relations people told them to tell. Truth was never to be the same again.

In the Falklands War it sometimes took longer for despatches to get back than in the Crimean War of more than a hundred years earlier, when the Dubliner, William Howard Russell, with his tent and his insect bites, told the true story about the incompetence of the generals and brought down the British government.

Following the Falklands War, the British Ministry of Defence commissioned the Centre for Journalism Studies at University College, Cardiff, to examine the problems in the relationship between the military and the media. During the war they had said that "the essence of successful warfare is secrecy, the essence of successful journalism is publicity", and they pretended that they now wanted to do something about it.

The noble, academic journalists produced a marvellous book, *The Fog of War*, and its 113 recommendations were mostly concerned with the public relations function[87]. So, what happened in the Gulf War ? The British and American military closed the loopholes which they had allowed, respectively, in the Falklands and the Vietnam wars and the public got even less truth.

The Gulf War was the first televised war, and for that reason some people thought they were getting close to the truth. But they were further than ever from it. Deception on a grand scale was carried out. Most of the journalists went with it, because they could not get access to any other source of news, so efficiently had the public relations machines of war managed to block them. Some, like Robert Fisk and Maggie O'Kane, went out on their own and brought back some of the truth.

The generals realised that they had to fight the war not only on the battlefronts in Saudi Arabia, Kuwait and Iraq but also on Ted Turner's Cable News Network. When they came on to speak about surgical bombing, and numbers of WIAs and KIAs and when they showed smiling, relaxed troops coming off a plane which had just bombed the Iraqis, they were not speaking off the cuff[88]. They were carefully rehearsed and prepared by their public relations people. Winning the war and justifying their reasons for being in the war was their objective; the truth could take care of itself and better if it didn't. Forget about the majority of the bombs which hit the unhappy people who were victims, rather than supporters, of Saddam Hussein and forget about the air crews whose nerves broke under the strain of what they were being asked to do.

It might be true to say that in war the first casualty is not truth, but the public relations profession, for it is responsible for the message that is allowed to be given to the journalists, and we learn about the war from the journalists.

And what about Northern Ireland, where groups of gangsters have spent more than twenty years killing their fellow countrymen ? Reading statements from the IRA and the UFF 'explaining' why they have killed people shows the depths to which public relations practice can descend.

If the truth were told in war what would happen ? Would the morale of the people be crushed ? Would even more young soldiers die? Or, would the war end sooner, once people saw the awfulness of what was being done on their name ? Would somebody shout stop ?

Perhaps the truth would end all wars, for did not Christ say that "the truth will make you free" (John 8:32).

Notes

1   *Quotations from Chairman Mao Tse-Tung*, Foreign Languages Press, Peking 1967, p. 300 ("The Little Red Book").
2   Ciaran Carty, *Robert Ballagh*, Magill, Dublin, 1986, p. 11
3   Ibid., p. 17
4   Edith Simmons quoted in *The Making of a Great Photo Opportunity*, The Guardian, 23 February 1988.
5   Ibid.
6   Quoted in *Charities 'have to give too'*, news report in *The Sunday Business Post*, 22 December 1991.
7   Desmond Roche, *The Civil Servant and Public Relations*, Administration, 11 (1963), p. 108.
8   Basil Chubb, *The Government and Politics of Ireland*, Longman, London, Second Edition, 1982, p. 326.
9   These regulations still apply . However, recent statements from the Minister for Defence make clear that he expects the Defence Forces to practice real public relations without the full rigour of these restraints.
10   They must have been very bright because they saw off the

public relations students from Rathmines in the first round !

11   Quoted by Carol Flynn in *Rag Trade Reaches out for Riches*, Marketing, March 1991.

12   Anita Roddick, *Body and Soul*, Ebury Press, London, 1991, p.9.

13   Ibid. p. 70.

14   Anonymous quote in Jane Lomas, *The Power of Presentation*, PR Week, 28 April 1988.

15   Roger Tredre, *Designers Say Shows Could be Out of Fashion*, The Independent, London, 20 March 1992.

16   Carol Flynn, *Rag Trade Reaches out for Riches*, Marketing, March 1991.

17   Mark Whittet, *Being Frank with Lynne*, PR Week, 18 February 1988.

18   Carol Flynn, *Marketing*, March 1991.

19   Fintan O'Toole, *GAA and the Burden of High Ideals*, Irish Times, 24 December 1991.

20   Paddy Downey, *The Blackest Day in GAA History*, Irish Times, 9 December 1991.

21   cf Sean Moran, *GAA Scores an Own Goal*, Sunday Tribune, 15 December 1991.

22   Sean Kilfeather, *GAA's new PRO should strive for Open Policy*. Irish Times, 21 May 1988.

23   Tomás Conlon, *The GAA's Central Defender*, Public Sector Times, May 1990.

24   Seán O Síocháin in interview with John Skehan on *Words and Music*, RTE Radio 1, 28 May 1992. O Síocháin was assistant general secretary of the GAA from 1946 to 1964, and then general secretary, later titled director general, until his retirement in 1979.

25   Martin Breheny, *GAA wants £7.5 million Sponsor for All-Irelands*, Sunday Press, 5 January 1992. The £7.5 million figure arrives from adding £1 million promotional costs a year to £1.5 million sponsorship money.

26   cf. RTE 1 Television programme, *Slants*, presented by Philip King, 8 December 1985.

27   Seamus Breathnach, *The Irish Police - from Earliest Times to the Present Day*, Anvil Press, Dublin, 1974, p. 191.

28   Frank Byrne, *An image cop-on by the gardai....*, Sunday Independent, 14 July 1985.

29   David Rice, *The Dragon's Brood*, HarperCollins, London, 1992.

30   Frank Byrne, op. cit.

31   Seamus Breathnach, op. cit., p. 186.

32   Frank Byrne, op. cit.

33   Quoted by Frank Byrne from *Garda Review*, 1985.

34   Frank Hanlon, *Dealing with the Press*, Garda Review, February 1989.

35   The Conroy Commission, Government Publications, Dublin, 1970, section 1261.

36   *Listener*, BBC London, 25 August 1966.

37   Steve Chibnall, *Law-And-Order News*, Tavistock Publications, London, 1977, p. 173. Report of speech by Robert Mark to Institute of Journalists in 1971 when he was Deputy Commissioner of Metropolitan Police, Scotland Yard.

38   Steve Chibnall, Ibid, p. 174, quoting internal Scotland yard memorandum, 24 May 1973.

39   Paul Holmes interview, *The Most Recognisable man in Public Relations*, PR World, August 1987.

40   John Waters, *The Fine Art of Fondling*, Sunday Independent, 23 April 1989.

41   Paul Mathieu review in *PR Week* (30 March 1989) of Mark Hertsgaard's *On Bended Knee., The Press and the Reagan Presidency*, Farrar Strauss Giroux, New York, 1988.. The phrase is lifted from Bill Shankly's description of Liverpool sports writers. The Hertsgaard book paints an uncomplimentary picture of public relations at the White House. It quotes deputy press secretary, Leslie Janka: "The whole thing was PR. This was a PR outfit that became president and took over the country. And the degree to which the constitution forced them to do things like make a budget, run policy and all that, (they) did. But their first, last and overarching activity was public relations".

42   Report in *PR Week*.

43   Heading to Stephen O'Byrne's report, *Irish Independent*, 24 October 1984.

44   The advisers to the Garret FitzGerald government, 1982-87,

o

were nicknamed 'The National Handlers'. Mara was quickly described as 'The National Fondler'.

45   Kevin Dawson, *Albert's Savage Soother,* Sunday Tribune, 29 March 1992.

46   Stephen Collins, *Tom Savage: What can he do to make you love the Government ?,* Sunday Press, 22 March 1992.

47   The enquiries into the beef industry, Greencore and Telecom Eireann in 1991 in the last days of Charles Haughey reminded many of the accident-prone Government of 1982. Stephen Collins, in *The Haughey File,* O'Brien Press, Dublin, 1992, describes GUBU: "The term GUBU was a joint invention of Haughey himself and his fiercest critic, Conor Cruise O'Brien. When a notorious murder suspect, Malcolm McArthur, was arrested in the flat of the Attorney General, Patrick Connolly, in the summer of 1982 Haughey described the situation as "grotesque, unbelievable, bizarre and unprecedented". Cruise O'Brien coined the acronym GUBU from the phrase and it came to signify the whole Haughey style of Government in 1982", p. 60.

48   Myles Tierney, *The Parish Pump,* Able Press, Dublin, 1982, p. 7.

49   Ibid. p. 7.

50   Quoted in Frank Kilfeather, *PRO for Dublin County Council urgently needed,* Irish Times, 23 October 1975.

51   Advertisements in *The Guardian,* for instance, during February 1990.

52   In interview with Kathy Myers, *The Guardian,* 25 November 1985, shortly after his appointment at the age of 32. He was elected MP for Hartlepool in the 1992 general election.

53   Scott M. Cutlip and Allen H. Center, *Effective Public Relations,* revised 5th ed., Prentice-Hall Inc, New Jersey, 1982.

54   Sam Black in Institute of Public Relations (ed), *A Guide to the Practice of Public Relations,* Newman Neame, London, 1958, p. 232.

55   J.Carroll Bateman, *Public Relations for the Business and Professional Association,* in Philip Lesly (ed), *The Handbook of Public Relations and Communications,* 4th edition, McGraw-Hill Book Company (UK), 1991, p. 557.

56   *Property Valuer,* Spring 1989.

57   Philip Baron, *Taking Account of Publicity*, PR Week 15 August 1991.

58   Quoted in James Morrissey, *Hot Whiskey - The Story of Ireland's Biggest ever Takeover Bid*, The Kerryman, Tralee, 1989, p. 186.

59   Ibid., p.62.

60   Quoted in Janet Izatt, *Opening a New Chapter in the Book Business*, PR Week 7 February 1991.

61   John Maher, *Irish Publishing is Balancing the Books*, Sunday Tribune, 14 October 1990.

62   Joan Plachta, *Diamonds are a Girl's Best Friend*, PR Week, 25 February 1988. Allen Jones had just won the Publishers Publicity Circle award for hardback fiction. Her new author, Sally Beauman came in at number one on the bestseller lists with *Destiny*.

63   Terry Mayer, *Public Relations for Retailers*, in Philip Lesly (ed),*The Handbook of Public Relations and Communications*, 4th Edition, McGraw-Hill Book Company (UK), p. 581.

64   Frank Jefkins, *Public Relations for your Business*, Mercury Books, London, 1987, p. 83.

65   Anita Roddick, *Body and Soul*, Ebury Press, London,, 1991, p. 220.

66   Lecture on *The Church and the Media* at a two-day seminar on aspects of Irish journalism, held at Cleraun Study Centre, Dublin, 22-23 February 1986. Bishop Comiskey was quoting from Report No. 21 of the Church's Council for Research and Development, Religious Beliefs, Practice and Moral Attitudes: A Comparison of two Irish Surveys 1974-1984.

67   Thomas J.M.Burke, SJ, in Walter M. Abbott, S.J. (Ed), *The Documents of Vatican 11*, Geoffrey Chapman, London, 1967, p. 317.

68   *Catholic Herald and Standard*, 15 August 1991. Quoted by Michael O'Toole in *More Kicks than Pence, a Life in Irish Journalism*, Poolbeg, Dublin, 1992. *Pray for the Wanderer,* Chapter 11 in O'Toole's book, deals with church and media.

69   Aileen O'Meara, *The Bishop vs. the Media*, The Sunday Tribune, 17 February 1991.

70   Pauline Madigan, DIT Graduate Diploma in Public Relations, Rathmines, 1992.

71   Quoted in John Feeney, *John Charles McQuaid, The Man and the Mask*, Mercier Press, Cork, 1974, p. 55.

72   Sean Lemass, *The Organisation behind the Economic Programme*, Administration 9, IPA, Dublin, 1961, p. 7. Quoted in Basil Chubb, *The Government and Politics of Ireland*, Second edition, Longman, London, 1982, p. 284.

73   The Devlin Report was the *Report of the Public Services Organisation Review Group, 1966-1969*, published in Dublin 1969. Liam St. John Devlin also chaired the Review Body on Higher Remunderation in the Public Sector which reported in 1972. At the time, this report was criticised, not so much for restraining public servants but for being too generous to some of them. As F.X.Carty wrote in *Business and Finance*, 21 December 1972: "Devlin's step-son, born last September at the cost of £58,000, got wide publicity for recommending higher pay for politicians, civil servants, judges and only some state-sponsored chief executives..... The new Devlin did not get a surfeit of bouquets in the public sector either because he started by admitting that 'there is no scientific method of determining pay' and then slotted everybody into a tidy place".

74   David Hanly, *In Guilt and in Glory*, Hutchinson, London, 1979, p. 16.

75   Daltún O Ceallaigh, *Trade Unions and the Mass Media.*, in Hugh Pollock (Ed), *Industrial Relations in Practice* (Issues in Industrial Relations 1), The O'Brien Press, Dublin, 1981, p. 139

76   cf. Report of the Executive Council 1990-91, ICTU.

77   Ibid. p.11.

78   Daltún O Ceallaigh, op. cit.,p.137.

79   Ibid. p.141.

80   Farrel Corcoran, Professor of Communications, Dublin City University, in *Learning Together*, Report of European Conference on joint research between trade unions, universities and third level education and research institutes, p. 42. The conference was organised in October 1990 by the Irish Congress of Trade Unions with the assistance of the European Communities.

81   Dr. Edward M. Walsh, *The Pursuit of Excellence and the Work Ethic*, University of Limerick News, no. 14, September 1991.

82   Patricia Palmer, *Apples, Arts, Amnesiacs and Emigrants: the*

University Connection, Irish Review, Cork University Press, Spring 1990, p. 16.

83   J.J.Lee, *Ireland 1912-1985*, Cambridge University Press, Cambridge, 1989, p.640.

84   Advertisement in *The Independent*, London, 18 June 1992.

85   Elaine Williams, *What's in a Name ? Changes in style and in resonance*, The Independent, London, 18 June 1992.

86   Michael Dummett, Wykeham Professor of Logic at Oxford University, in *The Tablet*, London, 19 June 1992.

87   Derrik Mercer, Geoff Mungham and Kevin Williams, *The Fog of War*, Heinemann, London, 1987.

88   WIA = Wounded in Action; KIA = Killed in Action.

P

Bibliography

Andrew, John; *How to Understand the Financial Press*, Kogan Page, London, 1990.

Arber, Katie; *The Practice of Public Relations*, Traverse-Healy & Regester Ltd, London, 1986.

Austin, Claire; *Successful Public Relations in a Week*, Hodder & Stoughton, London, 1992.

Baistow, Tom; *Fourth-Rate Estate, An Anatomy of Fleet Street*, Comedia Publishing Group, London, 1985.

Bayley, Edwin R; *Joe McCarthy and the Press*, University of Wisconsin Press, Wisconsin, 1980.

Bell, Quentin; *The PR Business*, Kogan Page, London, 1991.

Bernstein, David; *Company Image and Reality*, Holt Rinehart & Winston, New York, 1984.

Biddlecombe, Peter (ed); *Goodwill - The Wasted Asset*, Business Books, London, 1971.

Black, Sam & Sharpe, Melvin; *Practical Public Relations*, Prentice-Hall Inc., New Jersey, 1983.

Black, Sam; *Introduction to Public Relations*, Modino Press, London, 1989.

Bivins, Thomas; *Handbook for Public Relations Writing*, 2nd ed, NTC Business Books, Illinois, 1991.

Bland, Michael; *Be Your Own PR Man*, 2nd ed, Kogan Page, London, 1987.

Blond, Anthony; *The Book Book*, Jonathan Cape, London, 1985.

Blumenthal, L.Roy; *The Practice of Public Relations*, Macmillan, New York, 1972.

Bowman, Pat & Ellis, Nigel; *Manual of Public Relations*, Heinemann, London, 1977.

Bowman, Pat (ed); *Handbook of Financial Public Relations*, Heinemann, Oxford, 1989.

Bruce, Brendan; *Images of Power, How the Image Makers Shape our Leaders*, Kogan Page, London, 1992.

Burnett, Verne; *Solving Public Relations Problems*, B.C.Forbes & Son, New York, 1952.

Capper, Alan & Cunard, Peter; *The Public Relations Case Book*, Kogan Page, London, 1990.

Carlson, Julia; *Banned in Ireland - Censorship and the Irish Writer*, Routledge, London, 1990.

Chibnall, Steve; *Law-and-Order News - an Analysis of Crime Reporting in the British Press*, Tavistock Publications, London, 1977.

Cooney, John; *No News is Bad News, Communications Policy in the Catholic Church*, Veritas, Dublin, 1974.

Coulson Thomas, Colin; *Public Relations Problems - A Practical Guide*, Macdonald & Evans, London, 1979.

Coulson Thomas, Colin; *Public Relations is Your Business*, Business Books, London, 1981.

Cullen, Barry; *Commmunity Organisations and the Media*, Combat Poverty Agency, Dublin, 1989.

Cutlip, Scott M. & Center, Allen H; *Effective Public Relations*, revised 5th ed. Prentice-Hall Inc., New Jersey, 1982.

Dickinson, Sarah; *How to Take on the Media*, Weidenfeld & Nicolson, London, 1990.

Doty, Dorothy I; *Publicity and Public Relations*, Barron's Business Library, New York, 1990.

Downing, John and Mohammadi, Ali and Sreberny-Mohammadi, Annabelle; *Questioning the Media*, Sage Publications, London, 1990.

Drucker, Peter; *The Practice of Management*, Heinemann, London, 1955.

Ellis, Nigel; *Parliamentary Lobbying*, Heinemann, Oxford, 1989.

Evans, Harold; *Newsman's English*, Heinemann, London, 1972.

Greener, Tony; *The Secrets of Successful Public Relations and Image-Making*, Butterworth-Heinemann, Oxford, 1990.

Grunig, James & Hunt, Todd; *Managing Public Relations*, Holt Rinehart & Winston, New York, 1984.

Hamilton, Seymour; *A Communication Audit Handbook*, Pitman, London, 1987.

Harris, Robert; *Gotcha !, The Media, The Government and The Falklands Crisis*, Faber and Faber, London, 1983.

Harris, Thomas L; *The Marketer's Guide to Public Relations*, John Wiley & Sons Inc., New York, 1991.

Hart, Norman A.; *Effective Corporate Relations*, McGraw-Hill, London, 1987.

Haywood, Roger, *All about Public Relations*, 2nd ed, McGraw-Hill Book Company (UK), 1992.

Head, Victor (ed); *Successful Sponsorship*, Director Books, London, 1988.

Hertsgaard Mark; *On Bended Knee, The Press and the Reagan Presidency*, Farrar Strauss Giroux, New York, 1988.

Heylin, Angela; *Putting it Across, The Art of Communicating, Persuading and Presenting*, Michael Joseph, London, 1991.

Howard, Wilfred (ed); *The Practice of Public Relations*, Heinemann, London, 1982.

Hudson, Howard Penn; *Publishing Newsletters*, revised ed, Charles Scribner's Sons, New York, 1988.

Hurst, Bernice; *The Handbook of Communication Skills*, Guild Publishing (in arrangement with Kogan Page), London, 1991.

Ingham, Bernard; *Kill the Messenger*, HarperCollins, London, 1991.

Institute of Public Relations (ed); *A Guide to the Practice of Public Relations*, Newman Neame, London, 1958.

Jefkins, Frank, *Public Relations for Your Business*, Mercury Books, London, 1987.

Jefkins, Frank; *Public Relations Techniques*, Heinemann, London, 1988.

Jennings, Marie & Churchill, David; *Getting the Message Across, A Guide to Directing Corporate Communications*, Director Books, Cambridge, 1988.

Johnsson, Hans; *Professional Communications - for a Change*, Prentice-Hall (UK), London, 1990.

Knightley, Philip; *The First Casualty, The War Correspondent as Hero, Propagandist and Myth Maker*, revised ed, Quartet Books, London, 1982.

Kopel, E; *Financial & Corporate Public Relations*, McGraw-Hill, London, 1982.

Lesly, Philip (ed); *The Handbook of Public Relations and Communications*, 4th ed, McGraw-Hill Book Company (UK), 1991.

Lloyd, Herbert; *Teach Yourself Public Relations*, 3rd ed., Hodder & Stoughton, London, 1980.

McGinnis, Joe; *The Selling of the President 1968*, Andre Deutsch, London, 1970.

McQuail, Denis; *Mass Communication Theory, an Introduction;* Sage Publications, London, 1983.

MacShane, Denis; *Using the Media*, Pluto Press, London, 1979.

Mendes, Nicholas A. (ed); *This Public Relations Consultancy Business*, Nicholas Mendes & Associates, Halesowen, West Midlands, UK, 1984

Mercer, Derrik and Mungham, Geoff and Williams, Kevin; *The Fog of War, The Media on the Battlefield*, Heinemann, London, 1987.

Mercer, Laurie J. & Singer, Jennifer; *Opportunity Knocks: Using PR*, Chilton Book Company, Radnor, Pennsylvania, 1989.

Moore, H.Frazier H. & Canfield, Bertrand R.; *Public Relations - Principles, Cases and Problems*; 7th ed., Richard D. Irwin, Homewood, Illinois, 1977.

Morrissey, James; *Hot Whiskey - The Story of Ireland's Biggest Ever Takeover Bid*, The Kerryman, Tralee, 1989.

Moss, Danny (ed); *Public Relations in Practice, A Casebook*, Routledge, London, 1990.

Nally, Margaret (ed); *International Public Relations in Practice*, Kogan Page, London, 1992.

Newman, Karin; *Financial Marketing and Communications*, Holt, Rinehart and Winston, Eastbourne (UK), 1984.

O'Callaghan, Jerry; *The Red Book - The Hanrahan Case against Merck, Sharp and Dohme*, Poolbeg, Dublin, 1992.

O'Donnell, James D.; *How Ireland is Governed*, 6th ed. (reprint), Institute of Public Administration, Dublin, 1991.

Olasky, Marvin B; *Corporate Public Relations, A New Historical Perspective*, Laurence Erlbaum Associates, New Jersey,

1987.

Olins, Wally; *Corporate Identity*, Thames & Hudson, London, 1989.

Oram Hugh; *The Newspaper Book, A History of Newspapers in Ireland 1649-1983*, MO Books, Dublin, 1983.

O'Toole, Michael; *More Kicks than Pence - A Life in Irish Journalism*, Poolbeg, Dublin, 1992.

Oxley, Harold, *The Principles of Public Relations*, revised ed, Kogan Page, London, 1989.

Penn, Bill; *Be Your Own PR Expert*, Piatkus, London, 1992.

Pollock, Hugh (ed); *Industrial Relations in Practice*, The O'Brien Press, Dublin 1981.

Prone, Terry; *Do Your Own Publicity*, Poolbeg, Dublin, 1990.

Quinn, Feargal; *Crowning the Customer*, The O'Brien Press, Dublin, 1990.

Radio Telefís Eireann; *Broadcasting Guidelines for RTE Personnel*, RTE, Dublin, 1989.

Regester, Michael; *Crisis Management - What To Do When the Unthinkable Happens*; Business Books, London, 1989.

Roddick, Anita; *Body and Soul*, Ebury Press, London, 1991.

Simon, Raymond; *Public Relations Concepts and Practices*; 2nd ed., Grid Publihsing Inc., Columbus, Ohio, 1980.

Smith, N.Craig; *Morality and the Market*, Routledge, London, 1990.

Stephenson, Howard (ed); *Handbook of Public Relations*, 2nd ed., McGraw-Hill, New York, 1971.

Stone, Norman, *How to Manage Public Relations*, McGraw-Hill Book Company (UK), London, 1991.

Taylor, John; *War Photography, Realism in the British Press*, Routledge, London, 1991.

Taylor, Philip M; *War and the Media - Propaganda and Persuasion in the Gulf War*, Manchester University Press, Manchester, 1992.

Tierney, Martin; *The Media and How to Use it*, Veritas, Dublin, 1988.

Tierney, Myles; *The Parish Pump*, Able Press, Dublin, 1982.

Turner, Stuart; *Thorsons Guide to Public Relations*, Thorsons,

Wellingborough (UK), 1987.

White, Jon; *How to Understand and Manage Public Relations*, Business Books, London, 1991.

Williams, Francis; *Press, Parliament and People*, Heinemann, London, 1946.

Winner, Paul; *Effective PR Management*, Kogan Page, London, 1987.

Wood, Robert J (with Gunther,Max); *Confessions of a PR Man*, NAL Books, New York, 1988.

Woodman, Kieran; *Media Control in Ireland 1923-1983*, Galway University Press, Galway, 1985.

Wragg. David; *Public Relations for Sales and Marketing Management*, Kogan Page, London, 1987.

Yale, David R; *The Publicity Handbook*, Bantam Books, New York, 1982.

Periodicals

The two which this writer has found most helpful are:

PR Week, Haymarket Business Publications Ltd, 22 Lancaster Gate, London W2 3LP (Subscriptions: 3-4 Hardwick St, London EC1). Weekly, good for news about public relations, but weaker on features than some years ago.

Communication World, International Association of Business Communicators, One Hallidie Plaza, Suite 600, San Francisco, California 94102, USA. Monthly, to members of IABC. Good, broad selection of features.

Others:

Communication Briefings, 140 South Broadway, Pitman, New Jersey 08071, USA.

IPRA Review, International Public Relations Association, Case postale 126, CH-1211, Geneva 20, Switzerland.

IPR Journal, Institute of Public Relations, The Old Trading House, 15 Northburgh St, London EC1V OPR.

O'Dwyer's PR Services, J.R.O'Dwyer Co. Inc., 271 Madison Avenue, New York, NY 10157-0160. USA.

Public Relations Journal, Public Relations Society of America, 845

Third Ave, NY 10022, USA.
Public Relations News, 127 East 80th Street, New York, NY 10021.
    USA.
Public Relations Quarterly, 44 W.Market St, Rhinebeck, NY 12572,
    USA.
Public Relations Review, 7100 Baltimore Boulevard, College Road,
    Maryland 20740, USA.

Irish:

IMJ Marketing Journal, 6 Sandyford Park, Burton Hall Road,
    Leopardstown, Dublin 18.
Management, Marino House, 53 Glasthule Road, Sandycove, Co.
    Dublin.
Marketing, Pinjara, 1 Albert Park, Sandycove, Co. Dublin.
Marketing Opinion, 12 Magennis Place, Dublin 2.

Index